# Angler's Mail

## GUIDE TO
# BIG CARP FISHING

# Angler's Mail

## GUIDE TO

# BIG CARP FISHING

## ANDY LITTLE

*Consultant editor ROY WESTWOOD*

HAMLYN

## Acknowledgements

The author and editor would like to thank the following fishery managers for their help in shooting the pictures for this book: Jack Ashford, Peter Cockwill, Ron Felton, John Raison, Graham Rowles, Dennis Smale.

**All photographs by Roy Westwood.**

First published in 1988 by
The Hamlyn Publishing Group Limited,
a Division of The Octopus Publishing Group plc,
Michelin House, 81 Fulham Road,
London SW3 6RB.

ISBN 0 600 55709 X

Printed in Spain by Gráficas Estella, S.A.

# Contents

# THE CARP BOOM

The cunning carp casts a powerful spell over tens of thousands of British anglers but there's no mystery about its magnetism. *Cyprinus carpio* is quite simply the largest, most intelligent and hard fighting of our freshwater species. In the peak of condition, it is also a most handsome fish.

But the cult of the carp is not inspired by physical attraction alone. A mystique has grown up around the species that drives many anglers to spend every free moment on the bank pursuing a solitary monster. It can become an obsession, with the tension of the hunt spilling over to dominate thoughts and dreams.

Carp fishing has changed radically in the last decade. Modern techniques have made it possible for the specialist carp angler to devote himself exclusively to his quarry, knowing that when his indicator moves or there is a swirl at his floater, he is only seconds away from feeling the sensation of a large carp surging away with the bait.

Twenty-five years ago you were lucky to know of a water containing a double-figure carp, let alone how to go about catching one. Now, fish of 20lb are stocked from Scotland down to the South Coast. With the basic kit and a bag of boilies, in theory nothing should stand in the way of you catching a large fish. Some carp waters contain as many as 50 or 60 fish in the 20lb class. That stacks the odds very much in your favour. In addition, baits and tackle have undergone rapid transformation, to the point where they are almost guaranteed to catch a carp if you invest the time and effort.

## Hard to catch

But it's not all one-sided. On many well-stocked waters the carp have learned quickly too and remain incredibly hard to catch. If you accept the challenge of chasing these fish, you may end up counting the number of runs in a full season on the fingers of one hand!

Highly motivated carpmen meet that challenge by putting their fishing before everything else, including work, family and social life. Marriages have ended in the divorce court for the sake of a carp or two! Some dedicated carpmen only work full-time during the three month Close Season so that they can fish from June to March without any restrictions. Others have no job at all and spend the Close Season baiting up favourite hotspots or fish spotting. But few maintain this selfish lifestyle for long: they literally burn themselves out.

Clearly this is extremism. But if you're totally new to carp fishing it's as well to be aware that it can be habit-forming! The majority of carp anglers are more level-headed about their fishing and recognise that the real name of the game is enjoyment. Remembering that simple fact helps retain a true perspective.

## Success factors

What qualities are needed to achieve consistent success in carp fishing? There are no great obstacles to overcome on over-stocked waters where the carp are con-

**Opposite:** Cult fish with many thousands of admirers. A big carp stands out from the crowd as the ultimate challenge.

stantly hungry — a sound bait and rig will score easily enough. But on fisheries where the carp do not rely on anglers' bait to survive, then it's a totally different story. The skilful angler will always be in a success league of his own on the tougher waters.

There are four major factors involved in attaining consistently good results: watercraft, location, presentation and confidence.

## Watercraft

It is very difficult to teach anyone watercraft. You are either born with a hunting instinct or you're not. But the ability to steal up on a fish without it sensing that you're in the vicinity is vital.

**A**

## Location

Location is frequently something of a mystery. It's easy enough when the carp can be seen in clear water or where they make a habit of bow-waving, bubbling or leaping. But when there are no visible clues to their whereabouts then tracking them down only comes with experience. You almost need a sixth sense to know where they are at any particular time.

## Presentation

Having pinpointed the fish and used watercraft to move into position without spooking them, it's vital to present the bait in the right manner. Should you cast directly at the carp or plot their movements until such time as they can be ambushed? Is it better to bait up and get the carp feeding confidently before risking a hookbait? Would the hair-rig or a side-hooked bait be best? Are the fish more likely to be caught on a pop-up, bottom bait or floater? These are all crucial considerations and as you progress through this book you should gain the knowledge to make the right decisions.

## Confidence

Finally, without confidence you might as well pack up and go home. You must have belief in what you are doing. When all four factors come together then you will catch carp consistently. It is the dividing line between the successful carp angler

**The great equalisers**
The development of the hair-rig followed by the launch of commercially manufactured boilie baits brought carpfishing success within everybody's reach. Here's the recommended method for mounting a boilie with the hair trapped midway along the hook shank.

**A.** Hair tied from eye of hook with Nash hair bead to hold boilie in place and small piece of silicone rubber slid down hook length.
**B.** Push silicone over eye and halfway down shank. Slot baiting needle in concave end of hair bead and push through boilie.
**C.** Remove bead from end of baiting needle and withdraw through bait leaving boilie trapped on hair.

**B**

**C**

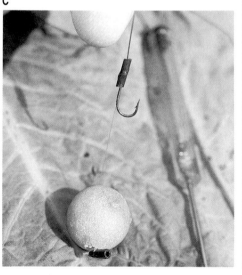

and the guy who hooks a fish occasionally but doesn't really know why he caught it.

## Glowing in winter

At one time carp were only hunted from the beginning of the season until November. It was considered almost impossible to catch them through the depths of winter because they hibernated. But the pioneers of winter carp-fishing demonstrated that this was a myth, and now carp lakes are just as productive in winter as in summer. On certain waters the fishing actually hots up!

It is true that carps' metabolism slows down in colder water but they certainly fight as hard as they do in summer, if not harder. Carp are in absolutely tip-top condition in winter. Their natural colours are enhanced and almost seem to glow. There's nothing quite as satisfying as capturing a big fish under extreme conditions, especially if there's snow underfoot!

## Types of carp

Although the carp was introduced into this country about 500 years ago, our knowledge of the species has remained scant until comparatively recent times. Originally, the carp were kept in monastery ponds, known as stews, as a food source. But there are few true descendants of these fish left today because the strain has been diluted.

### Wildies

True descendants of the original carp that do exist are called wildies and are chub-like in profile. The wildie has small, uniform scales covering its whole body and rarely exceeds 10lb in weight. Unless you know the stocking history of a particular water where they are reported to be present, then there is no guarantee that the fish are true wildies. The probability is that they are under-nourished common carp! The slow growth of wildies inspired selective breeding from faster growing fingerlings.

### King carp

The painstaking process of selection was repeated with wildies until the prolific king carp emerged. There are numerous strains of this with distinctive scale patterns. They fall into three groups which are popularly classified as common, leather and mirror carp.

*Common carp* have scales covering the entire body. They retain the same orderly scale pattern as the original wildie but have a more rotund body shape. *Leather carp*, also known as nude carp, have no scales whatsoever. *Mirror carp* have scales of various shapes and sizes, scattered haphazardly all over the body. There are also peculiarities among the mirrors such as the linear and fully-scaled mirror. The linear has two perfect rows of scales on each side of the body, one along the length of the lateral line and the other across the back just below the dorsal fin. The fully scaled mirror is similar to the common with scales covering its entire body but they are not of uniform size and shape. This latter scale pattern is probably the rarest of all.

## Food chains

King carp survive in just about every type of fishery, from fast flowing rivers and huge reservoirs to muddy canals and crystal clear gravel pits. They are extremely adaptable and are capable of capitalising on any food source that's going. They thrive best of all in a perfectly balanced water where the food chain is most abundant.

### Kings prefer pits

Gravel pits are the ideal location. Hundreds have been dug in the last 50 years and they usually boast excellent water quality and rich weed growth. The varying depth of the gravel seams results in a tremendous fluctuation in levels and the creation of bars and troughs in which debris accumulates to trigger the start of the food chain.

This type of environment is absolutely ideal for the chief dietary needs of the

**Above:** Two-tone common with uniform scale pattern. Carp displaying markedly different colour bands like this are relatively rare.

**Right:** Irregular scales dotted haphazardly over the body are the hallmark of the mirror.

carp such as bloodworm, shrimp and mussels. Providing the fish stocks are well balanced in a gravel pit, water clarity should be good for most of the time. But towards the end of the summer it is not unusual to see huge algae blooms turning the water into a pea green soup.

It is in lightly-stocked gravel pits that the very large carp are likely to be found. These fish may be 30 years old and will have grown to immense size on a natural diet. Catch one of these wily giants and you will have achieved the ultimate in carp fishing!

## Artificial lakes

A river that has been dammed to flood a river valley also provides a good basis on which to construct a carp lake but the result will be completely different in character to the gravel pit. The depth is likely to be more uniform and often quite shallow with a deeper channel running through the middle, marking the old river course. After heavy rain, these lakes colour up considerably which is good for the carp because extra food will be washed down from the riverbanks upstream.

**Left:** Brilliant example of a linear mirror with its neat row of scales running right along the lateral line.

**Below:** Scum of food blown in by the wind on a southern gravel pit. Just the sort of quiet bay where you'd expect carp to congregate on a blistering summer afternoon.

Weed growth on these waters varies depending on the amount of fertiliser used on the neighbouring farmland.

It is also possible to create a good carp fishery by introducing more fish than could be supported by the lake's food chain, and then sustaining the hungry stocks artificially with trout pellets. The growth rate on these waters is often much faster than on the natural, self-supporting lakes and pits. The instant carp fishery has been with us for some time and is sure to assume even greater importance in the future.

## Finding waters to fish

The opportunities to tackle good carp fisheries are within easy reach of everybody. Some of the cheapest fishing is available on local club cards or through commercial organisations such as Leisure Sport and Amey Anglers.

There are also syndicate waters but these are something of a closed shop. Access to them is more costly and often by personal invitation or recommendation. Every year sees an increase in the number of syndicated or season ticket waters, as derelict farm ponds and gravel pits are developed to cater for the carp boom. You will probably be paying anything up to £200 or more to join the more exclusive of these syndicates but it buys the privilege of fishing alongside a small team of anglers with the possible chance of a 30-pounder.

# THE COMPLETE CARP OUTFIT

You will never see me at the lakeside with all this equipment on the same day. I believe in travelling light otherwise mobility is sacrificed. But every single item of gear pictured here has been developed for a specific job, with the exception of the ice cream tubs!

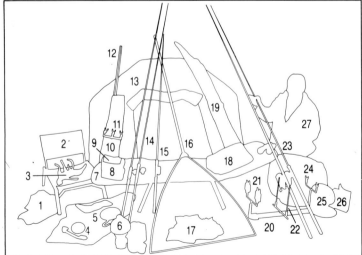

**1** Nash zip sacks to retain specimen carp for photography. They will hold any size of fish in complete safety as water passes freely through thousands of tiny holes in the weave. The carp cannot see out and there is no danger of it becoming distressed while held captive in the dark. A heavy duty, waterproof zip sewn along the side of the black sack makes it much easier to place fish inside than a drawstring. The sack Is tethered to a bank stick by a D ring and lanyard.

**2** Fox International low chair which is ideal for short sessions or stalking. Adjustable legs and anti-sink, swivel feet make it stable on uneven or soft banks. Replacement parts can be obtained for all the components.

**3** Feeding accessories to deal with different baits and distances. McCarthy *Pro-pult catapult* is for short-range baiting with boilies and for spraying particle baits. Wide gape aluminium frame with latex elastics and large pouch. Cobra swan-necked *throwing stick* to hurl hard, small diameter boilies up to 80 yards. Made from black anodised aluminium with rubber grip. Marksman's hunting *catapult* will fire boilies beyond 100 yards. Powerful latex elastics and slimline pouch. Gardner *Mixer Fixer*, a combined controller and bait dispenser for fishing particle floaters at long range. Gardner *Bait Rocket* also deposits particles or mini boilies beyond catapulting limits.

**4** Salter tubular spring balance. Made of brass; records up to 44lb in 8oz graduations. Nash weigh-sling with nose pouch and drawstrings suitable for weighing carp to 30lb.

**5** Nash dial scales record to 56lb in 4oz divisions. Moulded plastic design and very accurate. Used with Nash crescent-shaped, weighing bag which will cradle any size of carp.

**6** Tea-making equipment. Tubs hold teabags, sugar and powdered milk. Millets camping kettle and Colman petrol cooking-stove complete the field kitchen.

**7** Fox International Bowframe Bedchair. Heavy duty construction with adjustable legs. Positive locking system on the back frame. All four legs have swivel feet. Strong olive green canvas cover is foam-filled for extra comfort.

**8** Ice cream containers for odds and ends of tackle stack neatly in tackle bag.

**9** Optix Cormorant sunglasses with amber lenses to cut out surface glare.

**10** Nash stalking sling. Ideal for travelling light when moving from swim to swim. Holds umbrella, bank sticks and landing net. Comfortable shoulder strap.

**11** Custom-made buzzer bars engineered from high quality steel. These adjustable bars carry two or three rods.

**12** Spare rod for emergency use or to fling out the Bait Rocket.

**13** Nash 50in nylon brolly overwrap. Heavy duty nylon with built-in mud skirts. Double zip door has clear-view panel.

**14** Long range, 2$1/4$lb test curve rods. Custom-built 12ft Armalite blanks with abbreviated Duplon handles and Fuji FSP reel fitting. There are seven rings with the intermediates being single-leg Fuji silicone carbides. The butt is a three-legged model from the same range and the tip ring is 10mm diameter. These rods are teamed with Mitchell 300 reels which are ideal for long-range fishing because of their very even line lay.

**15** Jungle stalking stick. This is made from a North Western carp blank cut down to 8ft. The 20in butt has a Duplon handle and there are six heavy-duty, Fuji eyes. The test curve is about 2$3/4$lb.

**16** Dual mesh landing net with Gardner handle and Conoflex arms. There's a slot in the aluminium spreader block in which an isotope is glued for night fishing.

**17** Shelf-life Crafty Catcher boilies. The range includes King Prawn, Black Cherry, Caribbean Cocktail, Dairy Cream Fudge, Peanut Pro and Strawberry.

**18** Sleeping bag rated at 13 Tog. Full length, quick-release zip, built-in head bag and groundsheet. Waterproof overbag for monsoon weather.

**19** Nash Hooker holdall. Takes six rods — three of which can be already made up with reels — landing net, umbrella, bank sticks and buzzer bars. There's a full length nylon zip, carrying handle and shoulder strap.

**20** Gardner Rod Pod for hard or concrete banks which bank sticks will not penetrate.

**21** Super Compact Optonics with latching LED's plus volume and tone controls. Line travels over sensitive vane wheel which breaks a photo-electric cell to set off the alarm. They run on PP3 batteries.

**22** Monkey climb needles and bars. Custom-made from stainless steel. Indicators have flip-tops and milled slots for isotopes.

**23** Short- to medium-range rods. Tri-cast 1$3/4$lb test curve, through action blanks with full length Duplon handles and Fuji FSP reel fittings. Fuji silicone carbide rings throughout. Normally used with Abu Cardinal 55 reels for open bale arm fishing.

**24** Nash Rucksack takes everything — if you've got the back muscles to cope! Multitude of external pockets. Exceptionally robust.

**25** Bucket of peanuts flavoured with maple and sweeteners.

**26** Pedigree Chum Mixer. The most popular surface bait. It can be used straight from the box or soaked with colour and flavour.

**27** Hardy waterproof jacket.

# BEHAVIOUR & LOCATION

Knowledge of carp behaviour and their feeding habits, can provide many clues to their whereabouts and also when and how to catch them.

## Carps' natural diet

All kinds of aquatic animal make up the carp's diet in the wild but their favourite food is undoubtedly the midge larvae commonly known as bloodworm. Carp love to root in the bottom detritus and are superbly equipped to seek out bloodworm living in the mud. Another much preferred morsel is the dwarf pond snail or pea snail (*Limnaea truncatula*) which is plentiful in the weedy margins of many lakes and gravel pits. Whenever there's a population explosion of a favourite food such as bloodworm or pea snails, carp become preoccupied with it to the exclusion of everything else.

There are numerous other food items regularly cropped by carp which almost suggests that they have the ability to select a balanced diet. In addition, they often suck and slurp at three species of water plants: spiked water milfoil, broadleaf pond weed and Canadian pond weed. It is not known for certain if they actually eat the weed as the fibre element in their diet or if they simply suck at insects and other food forms living on the leaves.

Fish fry are a food source not widely associated with carp although they are obviously carnivorous and pike anglers have been known to hook them on live and dead baits. I also know of several that have seized plugs and spinners.

## Throat crushers

Carp do not have any teeth in their mouth; they crush up their food with a pair of bones in the throat called pharyngeals or pharyngeal teeth. These are very hard and strong and will easily crush items such as large freshwater swan mussels. When eating bloodworm, carp suck in great mouthfuls of mud along with the larvae, all of which is passed through to the gut. Once in the gut, the food source is broken down with the aid of enzymes into four categories: proteins, carbohydrates, fats or oils, and cellulose. The protein is converted to promote growth, while carbohydrates are an energy source and help with movement, breathing and heartbeat. The fats and oils serve as a back-up energy store but are chiefly responsible for weight increase. Finally, the cellulose with all the indigestible matter acts as roughage and is excreted. This is the basis of the carp's digestive system.

## Natural feeding zones

The carp's customary feeding zones are obviously found where there is the greatest concentration of natural food. At times, the preferred food item can be so abundant that the carp feed on it exclusively. For example, carp rooting through a large bed of bloodworm become preoccupied to the point where they are oblivious of any other food source that they come across. When this happens it follows that the carp are very difficult to catch.

**Opposite:** Deep in the jungle with a beast of a rod that's designed to beat any carp into instant submission. Hook and hold is the name of the game.

## Bloodworm beds

The most productive bloodworm beds will be visited very frequently by the carp and they'll send streams of bubbles to the surface as they set about getting their fill. Study this bubbling carefully and you'll eventually interpret what is happening down below by the size, pattern and speed at which the bubbles are moving.

On lakes and ponds, bloodworm beds are often extensive, and pinpoint accuracy is not essential. But this is not the case in gravel pits where the depths are variable. Here the bloodworm will almost certainly be found in the bottom of troughs among rotting debris. Some of the most productive channels might only be 1.25m (4ft) wide and the carp will regularly graze up and down them. Cast either side of the channel on the shallower bars and you won't get a fish.

## Shady spots

Carp also love feeding under the protective canopy of trees and bushes where they feel secure. Rotting vegetation in these shaded spots attracts plenty of insects but the food supplies are often quickly exhausted. A new feeding patch might be dirty for a time but once the bottom starts to appear much cleaner then the chances of hooking a fish are very good indeed. Ultimately the feeding patch will be swept completely clean by the carp leaving no natural food there at all. When that happens the carp depart and graze the bottom somewhere else.

It doesn't take many days for the cleanly swept patch to start filling up again with debris and the whole cycle is repeated. These natural hotspots can last for several weeks or for a whole season depending on the amount of food, numbers of carp and how often the fish are caught. But you can bet your life that as soon as one hotspot has gone cold a fresh one will emerge in another area of the lake.

## Weed beds

Weed beds are another environment liked by carp. They'll spend hours picking snails from the underside of lily pads and broad-leafed pond weed or browsing through dense strands of Canadian pond weed. When it's very hot they'll tend to bask in the middle of the weed and only give themselves away by venting or by the odd slurp. Basking carp are not inclined to feed ravenously and will only pick off the odd insect.

Other feeding areas include the mouths of streams or drainage ditches where the highly oxygenated water should be crammed with food.

## Artificial hotspots

The above are all natural feeding zones but it's also possible to create hotspots by introducing an unnatural food source. Quite often this happens almost by chance. For example, most anglers look for a clean bottom on which to fish their baits believing that a carp is more likely to find it than if it was cast among twigs, leaves and other debris. Constant baiting of the clean areas sets up a feeding zone. In gravel pits, these favoured spots tend to be on the tops of bars and shelves.

Artificial feeding zones are frequently created on lakes and ponds by anglers concentrating their efforts in favourite swims. This is particularly true when particle-type baits are regularly introduced. Hundreds of particles sink into the bottom silt and carp dig merrily away to find them. Artificial hotspots are not as consistently productive as the natural feeding zones. It is always preferable to present a bait to carp in an area where they are feeding naturally.

# Feeding times

The popular belief is that carp feed more vigorously at night but I've never found this to be true. Perhaps the main reason why the night myth has developed is because carp waters are generally quieter during the hours of darkness. The carp hunter is usually sound asleep and with no movement on the bank the carp are much more likely to venture into his swim. That gives the impression that carp feed more avidly at night.

Another misconception is that carp feed at specific times of the day or night and

Gravel pit shallows with a clean bottom. Constant baiting will contain the carp in a tight area like this even though the island margins are their natural territory.

only in the same areas of the lake. But in reality, once you've found the fish, they should be catchable whatever the time. It is more a question of presenting the bait correctly than waiting until the same time in the same swim where you have previously caught a fish.

The only period when feeding cycles do appear to become fixed is in the winter months. In cold, wintry conditions carp barely move a muscle for hour after hour. They're conserving their energy and may only feed for 1 hour in 24. At this time it may be just possible to set the clock by the carp's feeding pattern.

## Social behaviour

Carp are naturally shoal creatures. They enjoy a close, social life and on most waters the same small shoal of fish stay together. There will be times when the shoal breaks up and the fish disperse but they'll soon team up again. Carp rarely become loners. An odd fish might break away and go off on its own for a spell but it will soon return to the fold.

### Shoal size

A shoal will consist of between 6 and 20 fish depending on the number of carp in the water. Sometimes these shoals merge together; this usually coincides with an explosion of natural food. A change in weather conditions or the introduction of a new food source by anglers can have the same effect. It is common to see carp roaming around in small groups and the size of the fish doesn't seem to have any bearing on the number in the shoal. Indeed, it is not unusual to see one very large fish accompanied by half-a-dozen much smaller specimens.

## Carp calendar

Let's take a brief look at a year in the life of a carp. It is interesting to see how the changing seasons affect their behaviour and appearance.

### Spring and Summer

Carp rarely spawn during the coarse fishing Close Season in springtime because water temperatures seldom climb high enough to trigger the act. The end of June or early July is the prime time for spawning. This is the only time of year when carp can be positively sexed externally. For several weeks before and after spawning, the males exhibit spawning tubercles around the head, pectoral fins and gill covers. These tubercles are very rough to the touch and resemble thousands of grey-white spots.

Sexing females is slightly more difficult. There will be no sign of tubercles and if the gills, pectorals and head are smooth then the chances are that it's a female. The stomach should also appear reasonably plump and the flesh around the abdomen will feel fairly hard. Females also tend to be the larger specimens.

The spawning act usually happens in the shallowest part of the lake, especially where there is plentiful weed cover. Carp will also shed their eggs on trailing branches, underwater tree roots or even an immersed bramble bush. A single female is usually accompanied by four or five males and towards the climax of spawning the surface explodes as the males heave the heavy females from the water sending spray and weed flying in all directions. Finally, the female will shed her sticky eggs amid plumes of milt from the males. The fecundity of a single female is amazing. A mid-double fish can produce several million eggs. Each egg is about 1.5mm in diameter and transparent.

After the exertions of spawning, the carp are in poor shape with scales missing, body scratches and split fins. But in the warming, food-rich water through to late summer they'll quickly regain lost bodyweight and injuries will heal.

### Autumn and winter

In autumn, when day and night temperature differences are less marked, the carp feed for much longer periods. Weight gain is now at a peak and the fish are in tip-top condition.

With the onset of winter their body colours are as bright as a new penny. The carps' movements become more sluggish as water temperatures fall and feeding periods are more limited. They might even go without food for two or three days. But in any case they require much less sustenance to maintain bodyweight as they are nowhere near as active as earlier in the year. By the end of the winter there will be a slight weight reduction and the brilliant bodily sheen of autumn and early winter will have faded. They appear more grey and seem to have a thicker protective layer of mucus. But the condition is only temporary as, following the rigours of spawning, they'll build up once again.

## Fish spotting

There are other behaviour patterns largely peculiar to the carp which assist greatly in locating the fish.

### Leaping

Perhaps carps' most spectacular behaviour is their habit of leaping clear from the water and crashing back down again. I have watched the same carp repeatedly leap and then dive immediately to the bottom sending up streams of fizzing bubbles. It's possible these gymnasts crash into the bottom silt to disturb bloodworm and rush around to gobble them up while they are free swimming. Then once they have a great mouthful of mud and bloodworm the carp feel the need to clean their gill covers and they do this by leaping. Another possible explanation of leaping is that it is an attempt by the carp to rid itself of irritating parasites.

Leaping does not always coincide with feeding. I recall watching fish in a reservoir hurtling clear of the surface time after time in water 9m (30ft) deep and I do not believe they had sufficient time between leaps to grab mouthfuls of bloodworm from the bottom. Whatever the real reason behind this behaviour, well it's worth casting to a leaping fish because it often leads to a carp on the bank.

### Bow-waving

Bow-waving is another common sight as a fast moving fish leaves a bulge of water in its wake. This is usually caused by a carp fleeing from an area in which it no longer feels safe.

### Bubbling

Probably the most promising location pointer of all is bubbling. Sometimes a release of natural gases from the bottom is mistaken for a feeding fish but it's easy enough to tell the two apart. Carp will not bubble in the same spot for more than a few minutes at a time. More often than not they move along at a steady rate. The trick is to sit down and line up the bubbles with a marker on the far bank and see if the bubbles start to move. If they do, they're coming from a fish.

Three other species also have a habit of bubbling: pike, tench and bream. Pike release gases when they come into contact with the bottom in pursuit of prey or after they have actually seized their victim. That means pike bubbling is fairly short-lived. Tench are more delicate feeders than carp and emit tiny, pinhead size bubbles. Bream bubbles are most easily confused with carp but as shoal fish there'll be more of them.

Carp themselves are ravenous, enthusiastic feeders and it's not unusual to see them grubbing down several inches into the bottom as they sink their snouts into nourishing layers of rich, red bloodworm. Look for a steady stream of quite large bubbles breaking the surface and moving along at an even pace. If there are a few carp feeding together then it should be possible to pick out individual fish by their bubbling. The bubbles will splatter on the surface in lanes two or three feet apart. The largest and most active bubbling is usually caused by the biggest fish.

At other times a fish may send up a virtual soda-stream of bubbles in one spot and then go down again 3 to 6m (10 to 20ft) away in a different area. This suggests that the bloodworm beds are small, and scattered over the lake's bottom. Occasionally, you'll spot carp sticking their head and shoulders out of the water. I'm not sure what causes this behaviour but it is a sign that the fish is feeding hard on the bottom, possibly rising to the surface to swill out the gill rakers or for an extra burst of oxygen.

## Tenting

In shallow, weedy water carp often reveal their whereabouts by surface movement of the weed. This is known as tenting. What happens is that the carp rises in the water and lifts the dense weed a couple of inches above the surface. Also look for reeds parting as the carp barge through the underwater stalks.

## Margin patrolling

All these behaviour patterns are strong location pointers but if you can actually see the carp in clear water at close quarters, then even better. This is often possible on fairly featureless lakes which are not subjected to heavy angling pressure. The carp will tend to patrol the margins where food supplies are greatest and a stealthy approach can produce big fish from right under your feet. Where bankside disturbance is fairly constant, the carp get pushed out of the margins and patrol the fringes of islands instead.

Much of the behaviour outlined above suggests that carp are more inclined to graze the shallower swims than the deeps, but it is not quite as straightforward as that. Variables such as temperature and season must also be taken into account. Water temperature rises and falls a great deal faster in shallows. On a hot midsummer's day you're more likely to find the fish basking in a weedy bay with the water barely covering their backs than in a 6m (20ft) deep hole. It's thought that the deepest water in the lake will always offer the best chance of a run in winter. This is probably true but also bear in mind that several days of sunshine or warm winds can tempt carp to move into the slightly warmer shallows.

Way out in the middle of the lake is a slightly deeper channel marking the old course of a river. It's beyond casting range from the bank but chest waders put it within reach!

Brace of big mirrors hooked in the autumn when they're approaching the peak of condition.

Wind direction can also influence the movement of carp. In theory the windward bank should always fish best because the extra turbulence colours the water and dislodges food items. But this isn't the case on many waters where the carp soon learn that 2oz leads are all zooming at them from the same direction!

## Giants in rivers

These factors mentioned above concerning carp location principally apply to still waters but it would be wrong to overlook rivers where the big fish potential is by comparison largely uncharted. The Thames, Trent and Nene are the most prolific rivers and offer the chance of immaculate 20-pounders. I'm sure that 30-pounders also exist in all three waterways.

The lack of interest in river carp fishing is chiefly a reflection of the difficulty in tackling running water with traditional open bale-arm techniques. I have caught numbers of Thames carp from weirpools, fast flowing sidestreams and even the inhospitable tidal reaches as far down-river as Battersea.

Location of river carp is much the same sort of exercise as on still waters — they'll still show a liking for weed beds, islands and any underwater obstructions. But you can also add to that weirs, lock cuttings and warm water outlets. If the pressure gets too much on your favourite still water then turn to the rivers where there are many hundreds of 20lb carp that have never seen a hook!

## How carp learn

One final question before we move on to bait and tackle fundamentals — are carp intelligent? When compared with its body size, the carp has the largest brain of any freshwater fish but I do not believe that carp are capable of reasoning or thinking as we would understand it.

What makes them so difficult to catch is that they quickly learn by association. Carp anglers tend to use the same sort of approach continually and carp learn from this. Once they have been caught several times on a specific bait or method they become very suspicious and may even bolt from the swim at the sight of the bait colour they associate with danger. This is particularly true on waters where the carp do not rely on anglers' baits to survive.

In a well-balanced environment, heavy-handed pressure will make the carp extremely difficult to catch. I have actually seen a carp pick up a hookbait, prick itself and then stand on its nose and slowly rotate until the hook has come out. At no time during this episode did the indicator move. On another occasion I watched a carp suck in and blow out a rig 20 times without once pricking itself on the hook. So how often do carp mouth the baits without us knowing? I suspect we'd be amazed at the answer to that question!

The other side of the coin is that in heavily-stocked waters where carp rely on a diet of boilies or particles, they will be far more willing to take a chance on picking up a suspicious set-up. The only alternative is to starve. Respect the carp's inbred cunning but do not fall into the trap of crediting them with more intelligence than they truly possess.

# BAITS & PRESENTATION

The golden rule is to find the fish before wetting a line. After location the most important factors are presentation and bait choice. Never fish blind on a water where you can avoid it because you'll run the risk of tediously long blank spells if there are no carp in the vicinity. That might sound glaringly obvious but the fact is that many anglers go to enormous trouble and expense with their gear and baits only to blow it all by fishing in totally the wrong spots.

## Choice of hookbaits

Carp baits have become increasingly sophisticated over the seasons and the choice confronting the angler has expanded enormously to take in hundreds of different flavour and colour combinations. New, improved baits are being developed constantly as top carp men strive to keep one step ahead of the opposition. It is a highly competitive and secretive business but you don't need to be on the inside track to stay in the race. Carp are contrary creatures and quite often fall for the most orthodox of offerings. Don't forget that Britain's first 50-pounder fell to a single grain of corn after years of bombardment by exotic particles and boilies dripping with goodness!

*Natural baits*. The first category of baits to consider are the naturals. Maggots and worms are the most popular, but slugs, leaches and tadpoles have also caught their fair share of fish. *Convenience baits*. Then there are convenience baits on supermarket shelves, such as bread, cheese, salami and luncheon meat. *Particle or mass baits*. Equally potent on their day are tinned kidney beans and chick peas which fall into the category of particle baits. Dehydrated beans, pulses and nuts are also available. Indeed, a particle or mass bait, as it is called, can be anything from a grain of hemp or rape seed to a butter bean or Brazil nut. *Pastes*. Plain and simple pastes were probably the first specialised carp baits to be developed and the ingredients here range from powerful smelling catmeat to trout pellets, cheese and fish. *Boilies*. These are the most popular type of bait and are now described in more detail.

## Boilie benefits

The versatile and productive boilie has emerged as the nation's favourite bait because it allows us to target carp more positively and avoid unwanted species of fish. Proven ingredients include virtually every edible substance under the sun that can be ground down or freeze dried and then whisked up with eggs to form the boilie mix. Fish meals, meat meals, carbohydrates, vegetable proteins — they've all been used with varying degrees of success. This immediately begs the question: is it preferable to roll your own or buy commercially-made boilies in a bag?

### Home-made mixes

The advantage of producing home-made boilies is that you have complete control over the ingredients — but at a price. The

**Free-sliding floater**
**A.** Coloured Mixer with rig tube insert which allows it to be blown back up the line. Note the untrimmed knot end which is pushed up the tubing to secure the bait for casting.
**B.** How the rig rides in the water. If the carp blows out the bait it shoots up the line leaving the hook behind – hopefully pricking the inside of the mouth.

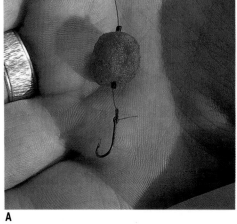

A

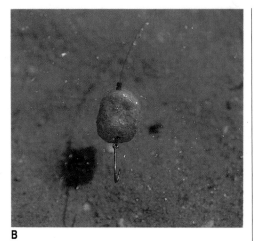

B

With neutral boilies you can wait until the last minute before deciding on the flavour of the day!

milk powders that make up a high-protein bait need to be purchased in bulk to be cost effective. This certainly applies to casein, calcium caseinate, lactalbumin and a calf milk substitute such as Vitameal. Bulking and binding ingredients such as soya isolate, soya flour and gluten are also best bought in bulk. Buying-in 25 kilo sacks of each of these ingredients means that some will be used up faster than others because a typical mix may contain 113gms (4oz) of casein but only 28gms (1oz) of lactalbumin.

Sharing the costs with a friend is the most economical way of purchasing these powders but if that's impossible then ready-packaged base mixes in smaller quantities are worth considering. These are more expensive and you will not be able to determine the ingredients but there are some excellent base mixtures on the market.

## Ready-made boilies

Shelf-life or frozen, ready-made boilies are the solution if you do not have the time or confidence to produce your own. There is a massive selection on sale including neutral boilies to which you can add your own colour and flavour. The arguments will probably persist for ever, but the satisfaction of landing a carp on a shelf-life boilie is no less than if it was hooked on a home-made special. Bait is only one small part of the jig-saw in successful carp hunting and I'm happy using commercial baits because it means more time spent on the bank instead of in the kitchen.

## Narrowing the choice

Faced with such a mountain of choice, from beans in a tin to packaged boilies, how do you narrow it all down to the right hookbait for the job? First, you must decide if you need a surface bait, bottom bait, or even a midwater bait. Obviously, there is little point in presenting a bottom bait in 10ft of water when most of the carp are cruising on top. That calls for a surface bait and the actual choice may hinge on what other kinds of fish, apart from carp, are present in the same swim. For example, rudd would tear apart a piece of floating crust in seconds and you'd need something more resistant such as a hard floating boilie or even a sunflower seed.

If there are a lot of carp on the surface it is tactically wrong to risk hooking one and spooking the rest. Far better to get them preoccupied on a mass floating bait before risking a cast. It's amazing how little notice carp take of a hooked fish in their midst when they're preoccupied and competing for a scattering of surface baits.

If there is a lone carp rather than a shoal then it is probably better to present a single floating bait. Catapulting out particles would give it too many snacks to choose from and that reduces your chances of a take.

On other occasions the carp may be swimming aimlessly through midwater showing no interest in surface or bottom offerings. These might be candidates for a slow sinking bait such as breadflake.

The choice of bottom baits is also dictated by other species present in the swim. If the carp are grossly outnumbered by bream and tench there'd be no point in fishing luncheon meat, sweetcorn or soft paste. A rock hard boilie or tiger nut would be required.

There is also a definite limit to the distance many baits can be fished. Under normal circumstances it is hopeless to try to fish a mass particle more than 30 metres out. At very long range — in excess of 100 metres — the only choice is a dense, hard boilie.

There are many waters where the carp won't look at a boilie, paste or particle because they have been caught on them too many times. At the other extreme, they might never have seen the baits before and ignore them as non-food items. In these cases, natural baits such as maggots, casters and lobworms come into their own.

It is wise to keep an open mind about baits and assess each water separately. If you are unable to visit a lake often enough to test individual baits you may well have to rely on local information. But make sure that it is supported by hard facts. Most carp anglers are prepared to name baits that have been successful in the past even if they are reluctant to reveal the going bait of the day. Knowing what has worked before will at least give you a good indication of where to start.

## Powers of attraction

After selecting the bait type, what about other factors such as its colour, smell, texture and size?

### Is colour important?

I do not believe colour is crucial although there are times when it is beneficial to pick a specific shade. For instance, on a hungry water where fish are competing for food, a brightly coloured and highly visual bait is an advantage. Conversely, where the fish are spooky in clear water it may prove necessary to camouflage the bait to make it inconspicuous and rely on smell as the chief attractor.

Colour is of no importance at all for surface baits because they all appear black when silhouetted on the surface against the sky. But colour-coded boilies are helpful for identification purposes. You'll find brown for maple and red for strawberry is a life-saver if the contents of packs get jumbled!

### Why smell matters

The carp detects a great deal of its food using its powerful sense of smell and every successful bait capitalises on this fact. Bread, cheese and meat owe most of their potency to smell. The majority of particles possess individual smells, some of which can't be bettered — maples, kidney beans and tiger nuts are good examples. Other particles such as black eyed beans, chick peas and haricots appear to work better with extra flavour added. As for boilies and pastes, the smell could almost

A

B

C

### How to flavour Chum Mixer

When carp become wary of floating dog biscuits, a dash of flavour can make a world of difference. Here's the most effective method.
**A.** Stir 10ml of the chosen flavour into a glass filled a quarter-full of water.
**B.** Pour the mixture into a plastic bag containing 1/2kg (1lb) of dry Mixer.
**C.** Blow air into bag and shake for several minutes until liquid is evenly distributed on Mixer. Leave overnight to ensure flavour completely penetrates the biscuits.

be considered essential whether it's a natural flavour along the lines of squid, yeast and liver or a synthetic such as Tutti Frutti, Dairy Cream Fudge or Hawaiian Tropical. With a natural flavour I do not believe the dosage is critical if you make your own baits. But synthetic flavours which could be concentrated by as much as 1,000 to 1 need watching. It is possible to exceed the flavour level to the point where the attractor becomes a repellant.

## Texture

At one time I used to go to great lengths to make sure all my bait ingredients were as finely ground as possible to produce a smooth, even-textured bait. But carp are well equipped to deal with very hard baits and actually enjoy chewing them. Now I believe in using baits which are harder and more granular in texture.

## Size

The optimum size for a bait differs widely. Carp readily feed on anything from the size of a pinhead to a tennis ball. When possible, I like to fish baits which are half an inch in diameter or less. Carp are more prepared to accept a bait of these dimensions than an unnatural looking offering the size of a tennis ball.

As a rule of thumb, the smaller the bait the more you'll need to introduce. There's little point in trying to trick a carp with a single grain of hemp or buckwheat. The possibility of it finding such a small morsel is very remote. But introduce an extensive carpet of the same bait, covering an area

1.2m (4ft) square, for example, and the chances are that several carp will move in and clean up every last grain.

But you can't apply the same principle to boilies. A single, 1in diameter boilie which is correctly flavoured will give off the same attractive smell as a whole bed of hemp, and the carp will react accordingly. The size of bait is also dictated by the range being fished. It is impossible to fish rape seed any further than a few yards from the bank whereas boilies can be catapulted over 100 metres.

## High-protein bait

Ultimately, the potential of a bait is generally considered to depend not so much on appearance or texture but on its protein content. Carp are thought to be capable of choosing between baits containing 70 per cent protein which do them a power of good and less satisfying mouthfuls with lower protein levels. That's the theory but it's really the same principle of carp learning by association. Over a period of time they get accustomed to picking up a certain type of bait and find they need to consume less of this food source to satisfy their bodily needs.

Unfortunately, this doesn't happen overnight and an intensive baiting campaign with a highly nutritious bait is easily undermined by somebody using a bait with the same smell but a considerably lower protein content. Food for thought there! Whatever you think about protein levels, the facts are that carp have been consistently caught on these baits for many years and they've shown improved growth rates. That's good enough reason for using them.

## Particle preoccupation

In the right hands, particles are one of the most devastating baits available. The essence of particle fishing is to substitute the carp's largest single item of food with your own chosen bait. When carried out correctly, it is possible to persuade the fish to preoccupy themselves with particles in much the same way as they would naturally feed exclusively on an abundance of bloodworm.

Usually, the smaller the particle the greater the degree of preoccupation. With small seeds such as hemp, rape and dari, you might need as much as 5lb of bait per fish in the swim at any one time and that could call for 30lb of bait carpeting a small area. If the particles are larger than about peanut size I do not believe it's possible to achieve a total state of preoccupation.

You will also find certain particles are more instant acting than others and so require less baiting up. The most instant ones are maples or mini-maples. Black-eyed beans and chick peas are also in this category although they seem to

work more effectively when flavoured.

The particle preoccupation has been taken to extremes on some waters, chiefly with tiger nuts and peanuts. What happens is that one or two anglers start catching well on these nuts and it has a knock-on effect. Soon everybody on the lake is fishing the same bait and it is just about impossible to catch carp on anything else. The lake's entire carp population becomes totally preoccupied with nuts. I do not like to hear of this occurring because it is detrimental to the well-being of the carp which needs a balanced diet to survive in the peak of condition.

On balance, the most consistent of the smaller particles over the seasons have been hemp, rape and dari seeds, and buckwheat. Middle-sized baits I'd recommend are tares, maples, chick peas, sweetcorn or maize, haricots and black-eyed beans. Among the larger particles, tiger nuts, peanuts and kidney beans have caught plenty of fish.

## Presentation

Presenting the bait in the right way is vital to success. The rigs described below have been divided into surface and bottom rigs, together with suitable baits and how to mount them. Finally, there are recommended rigs for fishing over silt and weed, and a more comprehensive list of leading bottom baits.

## Surface rigs and baits

For sheer excitement you can't beat catching carp off the top. A cube of crust is the oldest form of floater but these days a purpose-made cake is considered superior. The cake is made from the same ingredients as a bottom boilie but with twice as many eggs. The mixture is baked in the oven into a tough-skinned cake. But the most popular floating baits are dog and catfood biscuits. They are excellent carp catchers and are cheap and convenient to use with little or no preparation needed. Favourite brands include Chum Mixer, Meow Mix, Purina Sea Nip and

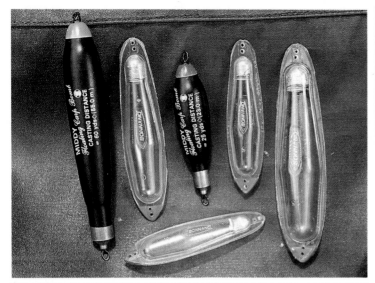

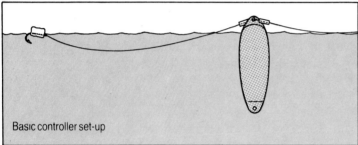

Basic controller set-up

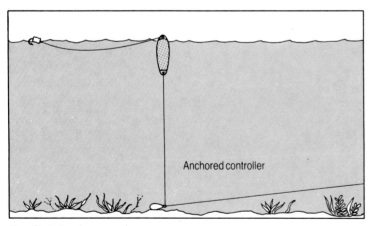

Anchored controller

**Top:** Controllers for staking out surface baits at short to middle ranges.

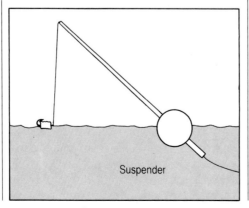

Suspender

Felix Meaty Crunch. Pet biscuits should be fished with a controller to provide casting weight.

## Fishing a controller

There are numerous commercially-made controllers but all function in the same manner. They are usually fitted with an eye or swivel at both ends and have a coloured top for visibility. A leaded bottom aids casting and cocks the controller.

A controller can be fixed on the line with a couple of stops. I prefer silicone rubber wedged in place with a piece of cocktail stick. I position a stop either side of the controller after passing the line through the top eye or swivel.

With a single floating particle, mount it on a hair or the shank of a size 10 or 12 hook. The length of the hook link must be a minimum of 0.6m (2ft) and when using a nylon trace make sure it's sunk below the surface otherwise carp will see it in silhouette and take fright. If the fish finally become wary of the sunken nylon, change to a dental floss hook length. The multi-stranded, waxed version marketed by Johnson and Johnson is fine. Once the floss is wet the strands separate out and resemble a soft stalk of weed floating on the surface.

If surface drift causes problems with the controller rig then a running lead will hold the bait in position. The lead is slid on first and the end of the line attached to the bottom eye of the controller with the hook link attached at the top. After casting out, line is released from the reel once it has been buried beneath the water to allow the controller to rise to the surface.

If the carp are really spooky and avoid a hookbait fished in this manner, the answer could be the Suspender. This is a controller with a difference — the hook length does not touch the water. The device consists of a long, rigid plastic tube with a polyball and counterbalance weight attached at the bottom. Line is passed through the centre of the tube and the hook tied at the end. The length of line between the hook and tip of the Suspender is carefully adjusted so no nylon rests on the surface. The Suspender is fished

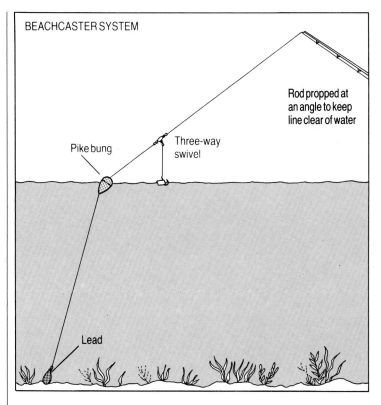

BEACHCASTER SYSTEM

Rod propped at an angle to keep line clear of water

Pike bung

Three-way swivel

Lead

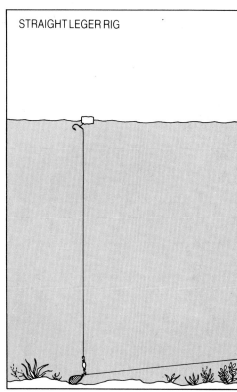

STRAIGHT LEGER RIG

on its own or with a running lead when drift or drag must be overcome.

## Beachcaster system

Another surface fishing set-up which avoids line touching the surface is the beachcaster rig. This effective method is restricted to waters no deeper than about 3m (10ft) or the length of your rod. A lead of 2oz or more is tied to the end of the main line and a pike bung or similar size float attached, to fish just over depth. The hook length is tied in about 0.6m (2ft) above the bung from a three-way swivel. Now the bait will sit on the surface with no line touching if the rod is propped up just off the vertical.

## Straight leger

A surface rig that can be used with just about any floating bait is a straightforward leger with the Arlesey bomb runnning directly on the main line and a hook length that corresponds exactly to the depth of the swim. Again, this rig can only be used in swims that are less than 3m (10ft) deep or it will be impossible to cast out.

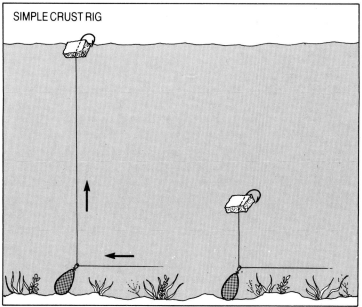

SIMPLE CRUST RIG

A similar method for depths greater than the length of the rod is the simple floating crust rig. The lead is totally free running and, as previously, line is buried and then released from the spool until the buoyant floater bobs to the surface. When stalking the margins or fishing at close range there is no need for any of these casting aids —the bait is freelined.

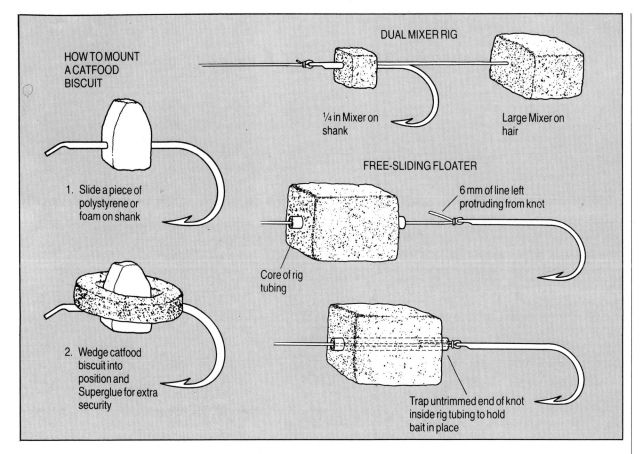

HOW TO MOUNT A CATFOOD BISCUIT

1. Slide a piece of polystyrene or foam on shank

2. Wedge catfood biscuit into position and Superglue for extra security

DUAL MIXER RIG

¼ in Mixer on shank

Large Mixer on hair

FREE-SLIDING FLOATER

6 mm of line left protruding from knot

Core of rig tubing

Trap untrimmed end of knot inside rig tubing to hold bait in place

### Mounting surface baits

Attaching crust and floating cake to the hook is a simple matter. The hook is pushed clean through the bait and out the other side leaving the point exposed for effective penetration. Floating boilies are normally best fished side-hooked or with a short hair.

Hard floating-particles are probably the most difficult to mount, especially if a single biscuit is not sufficiently buoyant to suspend the hook. With round, Polo-shaped catfood biscuits the answer is to slide a slither of polystyrene or foam on the bend of the hook. Then the biscuit can be wedged on this and if necessary held secure with Superglue.

The most widely used surface particle, Chum Mixer, is buoyant enough to fish directly on the shank of the hook or from a short hair. These round biscuits should be soaked beforehand to make them easier to mount — a needle sharp hook will blunt very quickly if you attempt to force it through a crunchy Mixer. A crafty rig idea for this bait is to mount a quarter piece of Mixer on the eye of a size 10 or 12 hook and then attach the largest biscuit you can find in the box to a long hair. Carp often swirl at Mixer to try to break it up before taking down the smaller pieces and this rig simulates that situation.

Sometimes carp suck in and blow out a particle floater faster than the human eye can see. This habit often develops when they've been caught frequently on baits such as Mixer, and for a period they will appear almost impossible to catch on conventional rigs. That's the moment to step in with a free-sliding surface bait. The idea is that the carp blows the bait back up the line but the hook is left trailing behind with a good chance that it will prick the fish in the lip. To construct this rig you'll need to push a short piece of small diameter rig tubing through the centre of the bait. This is easily done by first boring a hole through the bait with a drill bit or something similar. The tubing is then inserted leaving a short piece protruding either side of the floater. Slide the bait up the hooklink and tie on the hook, taking care to leave an untrimmed end of at least 6mm ($^1$/2in). This untrimmed piece is tucked back inside the rig tubing to prevent the bait flying up the line prematurely on the cast. One final point: if you fish the sliding Mixer rig with a controller, you will achieve a better strike rate.

Other floaters worth considering are breakfast cereals such as Sugar Puffs, Puffed Wheat and Start. They are all very effective on their day. Floating cake-type baits are obviously highly individual but some of the most consistently successful flavours you can add are brandy, strawberry and clove. Other longtime favourites include floating trout pellets and marshmallows.

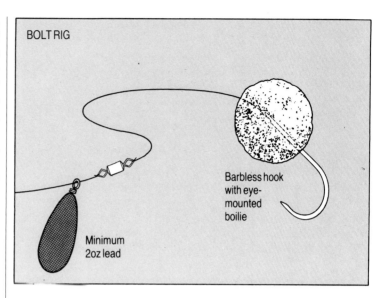

BOLT RIG

Barbless hook with eye-mounted boilie

Minimum 2oz lead

## Bottom rigs and baits

In the days of soft paste baits all you did was mould a chunk around the hook. A strong strike easily pulled the hook free of the bait and into the carp's mouth. This remained the case even when pads of crust and spaghetti were used on the bend of the hook to stop pastes flying off on a hard cast.

Then some forward thinking anglers decided to roll their baits in little balls and boil them for a few minutes to give a tough outer skin. The main reason for doing this was to stop nuisance fish attacking and whittling away the more vulnerable paste baits. These new skinned baits were fine as deterrents against unwanted small fish but it was just about impossible to heave a hook through them on the strike. In those early days of the boilie it was thought that carp would spook at the sight or feel of an exposed hook. We now know this is untrue, but it's funny to look back and remember the blistering runs we used to get on large, freelined skinned baits. You had to strike repeatedly to hook the carp and we didn't really have a hope.

Gradually, anglers started mounting baits with the point and bend of the hook exposed and the emergence of the side-hooked boilie was the first of the self-hooking rigs as we know them today. These side-hooked baits were originally

used with over 0.6m (2ft)-long hooklinks but they were soon shortened to a more effective length of 30-35cm (12-14in).

It was observed that a side-hooked boilie fished with a front clip on the rod to combat drift produced much faster takes and a bigger percentage of fish on the bank. The hook on this rig also started to get larger with more of it exposed. I suppose this was really the start of the bolt rig.

### Bolt rig

A true bolt rig comprises a short hooklink between 12.5-17.5cm (5-7in), with a very large, barbless, needle-sharp hook. The best hook is a Mustad Viking 94845 in size 1 and 2. These are a fine wire, forged barbless pattern with a down-turned tapered ball eye. A half-inch diameter boilie is mounted directly on the eye and a heavy lead of 2oz or more must be used with the line tightly clipped up. When the carp sucks in the bait and bolts on feeling the lead, the hook drives itself home.

### Hair-rig: how it works

Lennie Middleton's hair-rig rates as one of the greatest carp fishing advances in modern times. The rig was originally believed to work on a confidence principle. It was thought carp sucked in the bait two or three times and the hair-rig gave it the confidence to take it right back to the pharyngeal teeth. In reality this is not the

## Seven ways to present a bait

**1.** Counterbalanced rig for snaggy swims. **A.** The hook is made to float with a blob of foam on the bend. Hair-mounted bait is tied directly to the eye. **B.** When balanced out correctly the hook floats directly above the bait. The pattern is a size 4 Super Specimen tied to 15lb dental floss.

**2.** Sliding pop-up. **A.** Highly successful rig which allows the ring with its hair-mounted boilie to be free running between the hook and counterbalancing split-shot. To make a ring simply cut the eye off a suitable sized hook. **B.** Once the rig is sucked in and then ejected, the bait slides up the hook link leaving the size 10 Super Specimen hook inside the carp's mouth.

**3.** Bean or nut rig. Dacron hook link and hair with a size 10 Carp Catcher hook based on the Yorkshire Sedge pattern. There is no guarantee which way round the bait will be taken in and this shape of hook seems to cope best. The Brazil has been soft boiled allowing the use of a hair bead.

**1–A**

**1–B**

**2–A**

**2–B**

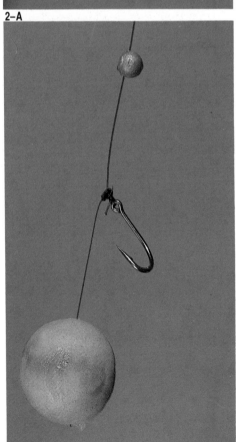

**3**

**5**

**7**

**4**

**6**

**4.** Double bait presentation. Quartered boilies are used here as particles but you could use one buoyant bait with the other being a sinker. The rig consists of a double looped hair about 7.5cm (3in) long which is slid through small bored rig tubing and down over the eye of the hook as shown. The baits are secured with Nash hair stops and the rig can be adjusted so one end is longer than the other if required. This rig's a winner with a mass type bait.

**5.** Side-hooked boilie. The first in a long line of self-hooking rigs. On waters where the hair-rig is not so efficient, the side-hooked bait with a hook link of between 9-12in is back in favour.

**6.** Standard hair. When using a Dacron hook link, it can be carried through the eye of the hook to form the hair.

**7.** Eye-mounted boilie. Another hugely successful method when fished with a heavy lead of 2oz and a short hook link of 12.5-17.5cm (5-7in). The lead is fixed or clipped up tightly and the hook size to boilie ratio is approximately a half-inch boilie to a size 2 hook. The hook, normally barbless, is honed to a needle point. Once the bait is picked up, the fish is pricked and bolts against the fixed lead or line clip producing a screaming take.

case. The hair-rig is simply a highly effective self-hooking method. With the hair there's a much greater chance of the free hook actually catching on a fleshy part inside the carp's mouth.

The rig has been a great equaliser in carp fishing. Before it emerged, the angler who invested a lot of effort in positioning the bait in exactly the right place on the hook and worked out the most efficient length of hooklink caught a lot more fish. But when details of the hair circulated it was was no longer so critical to get these parameters right. You could get just as many runs on a 6cm (2.5in) hair as with a 2.5cm (1in) hair or less. Then, after a couple of years the carp started to avoid more clumsily presented hair rigs. Once again they had learned by association.

### Attaching the hair

The original hair-rig set-up consisted of a hooklink of less than 0.6m (2ft) with a size 4 hook and a hair of 5-7.5cm (2-3in). attached to the bend of the hook. There have been all manner of changes but it is now recognised that there are three parts of the hook on which the hair can be attached with a bottom bait. These are: from the eye, off the bend, and along the shank. Which of these is most effective? Probably the clearest way of assessing this is to look at each method.

A hair attached to the *bend of the hook* will definitely be sucked in the right way but when blown out the hook will be turned in the mouth and emerge the wrong way with little chance of pricking the fish. A hair swinging *from the eye* of the hook will be fine when blown out. The bait will probably have the effect of aiding the pricking of the hook, as it is ejected quite fast forcing the point home. But what about when it is sucked in? There is a chance here that the hook could go in eye first, possibly causing it to catch on the outside of the mouth or even fail to enter at all. By fat the most efficient place to attach the hair is halfway *along the shank* This ensures that the hook goes in the carp's mouth, bend first. When ejected it will pivot round trying to force the hook out, eye first. That gives an excellent chance of the point pricking in the carp's mouth.

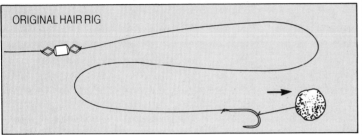

ORIGINAL HAIR RIG

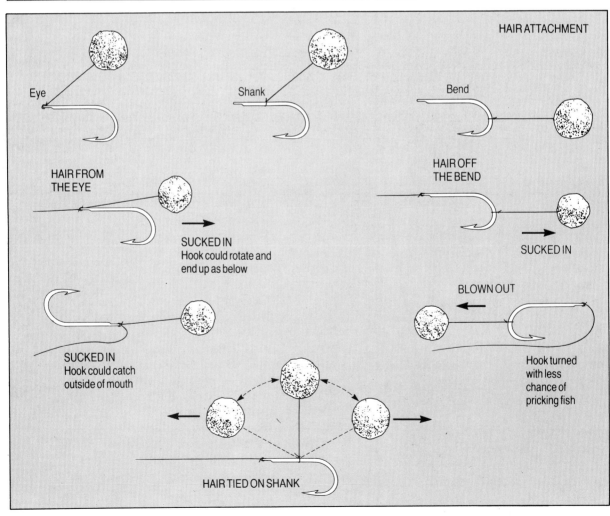

HAIR ATTACHMENT

Eye

Shank

Bend

HAIR FROM THE EYE

HAIR OFF THE BEND

SUCKED IN
Hook could rotate and end up as below

SUCKED IN

SUCKED IN
Hook could catch outside of mouth

BLOWN OUT

Hook turned with less chance of pricking fish

HAIR TIED ON SHANK

A good hook for this rig is the Drennan Super Specialist. It is fairly wide in the gape, has a chemically sharpened point and is constructed on strong wire. Consider the alternatives. A pattern with a turned out point will probably prick the fish but it could roll over and pull out as the pressure increases. An inturned point gives a better hook-hold, actually winding itself into the flesh, but it is not nearly as good at self-pricking. It's for these reasons that I have settled for a straight point hook such as the Super Specialist.

The best method of constructing a hair rig is to tie the hair to the eye of the hook — sounds contradictory I know! — then slide a small piece of silicone rubber down the hooklink. Feed the rubber over the eye of the hook and trap the hair in exactly the right position on the shank.

The hair itself can be a length of 1lb Dacron which is very supple and allows the bait to move freely in an arc inside the carp's mouth with less chance of it pulling the hook out of line. The drawback with this material is that it breaks very easily. If that causes you problems, try separating the strands of unwaxed dental floss —a single strand has a breaking strain of about 4lb.

After exclusive experiments I have found that a hair length of about 2cm (3/4in) between the bait and hook is the most consistent catcher.

*Hair stops and beads.* There are numerous ways of trapping the bait on a hair.

Kevin Nash beads and stops are the easiest and most efficient way in my experience. The plastic beads are hollowed out at one end to take a purpose-made, blunt-ended baiting needle and there is a small hole at the other end through which the hair is tied. It's a simple operation to push the bead and hair through the bait with the needle and then withdraw it leaving the boilie hanging on the hair.

With the Nash stop, a small loop is tied in the end of the hair and pulled through the bait with a slender 0. 75 crochet hook. Then the dumbell-shaped hair stop is trapped in the loop against the bait, holding it firmly in place on the hair.

You can use the beads with all bottom

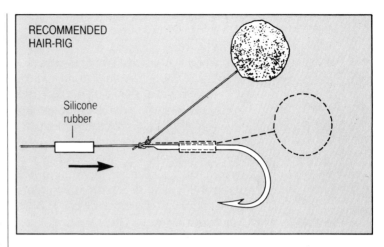

RECOMMENDED HAIR-RIG

Silicone rubber

boilies and soft particles while the hair stops are a better choice for pop-ups and harder particles. The crochet needle is slightly smaller in diameter than the hair bead and doesn't damage the outer skin of the pop-up quite as much. That means there is less danger of the bait becoming waterlogged and sinking to the bottom. It is also easier to use a crochet hook with hard particles because forcing a bead through a hard bait soon loosens the knot attaching it to the hair.

*Hook lengths.* For the hook length, the

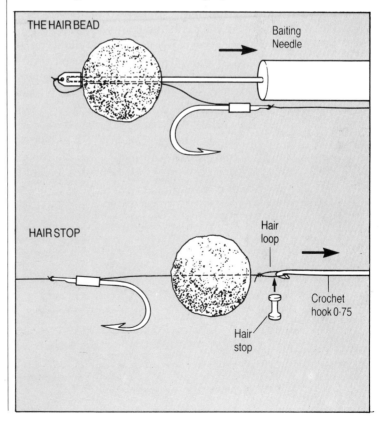

THE HAIR BEAD

Baiting Needle

HAIR STOP

Hair loop

Crochet hook 0·75

Hair stop

leading materials are nylon, dental floss and Dacron. Where links of 4-8lb are required, nylon is first choice as there is no great advantage in using any other material in these lower breaking strains. Dental floss breaks at around 12lb so that's the next step up. Recommended brands are Johnson and Johnson, Sensodyne and Superdrug. In heavily weeded or snaggy swims, Dacron of 15-20lb is used as the situation dictates. Providing you are not fishing over too silty a bottom, start off with a hooklink of about 30cm (12in). Lengthen it if you feel the carp hasn't got sufficient leeway to suck the bait in freely, or shorten it if it blows out without the fish pricking itself. The length of the hooklink should not be shorter than 22cm (9in) or longer than 45cm (18in) when fished with the hair-rig.

### Attaching hooks and swivels

Tying on hooks and swivels to hook traces demands great care. It is important to saturate the knot with saliva so that the coils bed down without burning or excessive constriction. I use a five-turn blood knot for nylon links but Dacron and dental floss only require two or three turns. Any will make the knot unreliable.

The blood knot is the most reliable knot in fishing whatever anybody else tells you! I use it for attaching all hooks and swivels to nylon line. The tying sequence is simple. Pass the end of the line through the eye of the hook and wrap the loose end around the main line five times before feeding it back through the first loop formed nearest the eye. Moisten the knot before drawing tight.

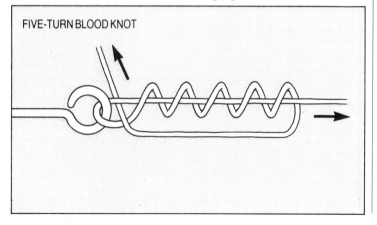

FIVE-TURN BLOOD KNOT

This same knot can also be tied at night in the pitch black without too much fumbling. The line is passed through the eye by holding the hook on the tip of the tongue and prodding with the end of the line until the hole is located. Once the hook or swivel has been slid on the line, leave a longer loose end than usual. Then insert a finger against the eye and form a loop behind it, turning the loose end five times around the main line. Finally, feel for the loose end through the loop created by your finger and tighten down.

### Pop-up rig

A bottom rig with great potential on many waters is the pop-up which I usually fish somewhere between 5-22cm (2-9in) clear of the bottom.

Pop-ups are floaters made in exactly the same way as normal boilies but cooked in a microwave or oven to create a watertight skin. Shop-bought boilies can be made to float by grilling but they need to be turned very carefully so the skin forms right around the bait.

An emergency method for making a pop-up if you find yourself on the bank without any floaters, is to insert a small polyball or piece of rig foam in the middle of the bait. This is quite easily done by slicing off the top of the boilie with a sharp knife or razor blade, boring out the centre with a drill, inserting the polyball and Supergluing the top back on again. It sounds incredibly tricky but the picture sequence demonstrates it's a simple process. Incidentally, the pop-up polyboilie has the advantage of not losing any of the flavour as happens with oven or microwaved baits.

The idea behind the pop-up rig is that when a carp swims into a baited area the pop-up bait is the most prominent and so more likely to be taken first. I usually counter-balance the pop-up with a splitshot — a BB is about right — which is just sufficient to tether it the required distance above the bottom. When the fish are feeding ravenously and bouncing baits several inches off the bottom in their eagerness to get their fill, then try fishing the pop-up directly off the lead. A boilie suspended about 22cm (9in) above the bed of the

**A**

**B**

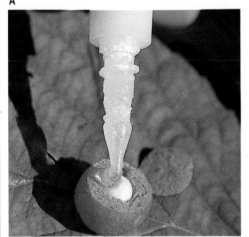

**C**

**D**

**Emergency pop-up**
If you leave your floaters at home but want to fish a pop-up, then give a bottom boilie the polyball treatment as follows.
**A.** Slice the top off a boilie and drill out the centre.
**B.** Insert a polyball – they're sold as bean bag fillers.
**C.** Slightly moisten the two surfaces of the cut boilie and Superglue them back together again.
**D.** The finished job.

lake in these situations guarantees the carp will find it.

With boilies counter-balanced by a split-shot, I use two different pop-up rigs. One is much the same as the off-the-shank hair-rig with about a .75in hair. The other is a sliding hair tied to the cut-off eye of a Jack Hilton carp-hook. The eye slides between the counterbalance split-shot and the hook, and when ejected the bait flies out of the mouth leaving the lightly pricked hook behind.

## Particle rigs

The mini-particles, including hemp, cannot be fished effectively as single grains on carp tackle. The best method is to Superglue 10 to 15 seeds along a dental floss hair, leaving .75in between the hook and the first seed.

Medium-size particles, such as maples, can be fished on a hair in ones and twos while larger black-eyed beans and peanuts are presented singly. It is also feasible to

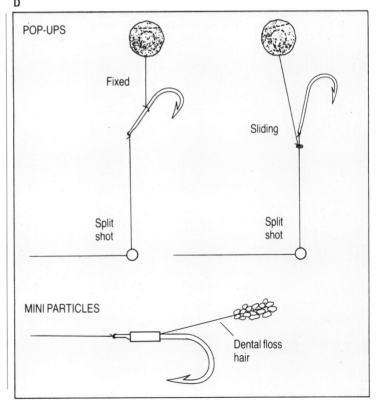

POP-UPS

Fixed

Sliding

Split shot

Split shot

MINI PARTICLES

Dental floss hair

offer these larger nuts as pop-ups by inserting polystyrene inside in the same way as the polyball offerings described under the pop-up rig.

When carp really get down to eating the particles they will take a hookbait as though it was a free offering. This might result in the bait and hooklink passing right back over the pharyngeal teeth causing a phenomenon known as the bite-off. The carp swallows the hook and you lose the fish. To avoid this, limit the length of the hooklink to 22cm (9in). It is probably best fished with a lead over 2oz either semi-fixed or clipped up. That should ensure that the carp bolts on feeling the lead and doesn't take the bait deep down.

If bite-offs persist after taking these precautions, then resort to a frightener on the line. Using a needle, thread the hooklink

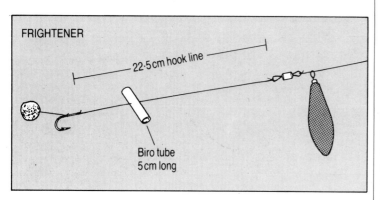

FRIGHTENER

22·5cm hook line

Biro tube 5cm long

through 5cm (2in) of plastic biro tube and Superglue it in position about 7.5cm (3in) from the hook. The tube will hit the carp's mouth when the hookbait is sucked in causing it to panic and probably hook itself in the process.

## Leger stops and weights

For 90 per cent of my legering rigs I use a swivel to stop the lead running down to the hook. It's the most reliable method and absorbs the stress of constant casting better than the plugged tube stops which weaken the rig by pinching the nylon. I've found Berkley and Kevin Nash swivels reliable in size 8 to 10 with round or diamond eyes. As an extra precaution, slip on a bead between the lead and swivel to act as a shock absorber.

The leger weights are mostly straight

copies of Dick Walker's original aerodynamic Arlesey bomb with a swivel at one end. Where there is a total lead ban, substitute zinc weights work equally satisfactorily. Stock up with an assortment of bombs between 0.5oz and 3oz in half-ounce graduations and you'll meet most demands in carp fishing.

## Anti-tangle rigs

Soft hooklinks of dental floss and Dacron really require the lead to be fished with an anti-tangle system. Four favourites are:

*Weed and silt bottoms.* This rig consists of a length of stiff tubing with a bead and swivel mounted at one end. The lead can be attached directly to the swivel or on a link of nylon which is adjusted to correspond with the depth of weed or silt. Essentially it is a free-running rig, but the tubing can be wedged against the hooklink swivel with a piece of cocktail stick if you want to fish it fixed.

*Hard bottoms.* A distinctly different rig, with the lead mounted directly on a stiff

A

B

### How to fish a semi-fixed lead

**Far Left:**
The wrong way. If you hang the bomb from the eye of a swivel it could finish up permanently tethered to a carp.

**Left:**
**A.** Much better. Slide the lead over the eye of the swivel and wedge it in place with a plug of latex cut from a catapult.
**B.** If the line should break above the bomb then the weight easily pulls free over the elastic.

**Below:**
**A.** Alternative method with flexible tubing and bead.
**B.** No problem in the event of a break – the carp can jettison the bomb.

A

B

ANTI-TANGLE SYSTEMS

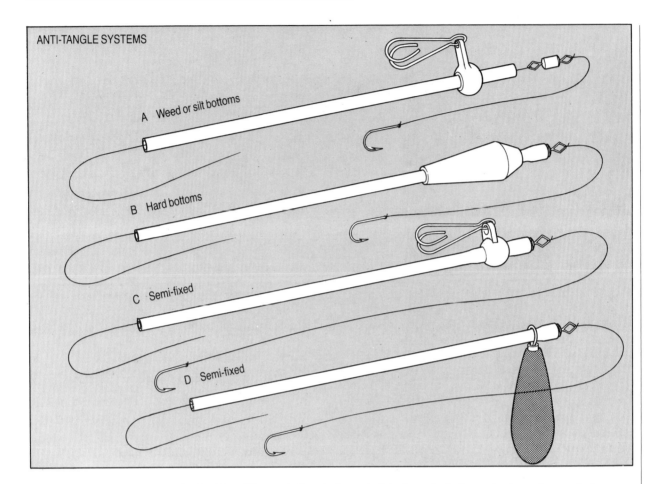

A Weed or silt bottoms

B Hard bottoms

C Semi-fixed

D Semi-fixed

length of tubing. The main line is threaded through the tube and the hooklink attached. This is another running rig that can be stopped with a piece of cocktail stick.

*Semi-fixed rigs.* There are two types of semi-fixed rigs:

In the first, the chief component is a length of flexible Kevin Nash 2mm rig tubing together with a bolt bead from the same manufacturer. One side of the bead has a spigot on which the rig tubing is pushed. A slightly smaller spigot protrudes from the other side of the bead and this takes a short length of the next-size-down rig-tubing which is also pushed over the stop swivel. This serves as a fixed lead but if it snags up, the hooklink can be freely pulled out. The bolt bead also carries the lead on a link swivel. The second rig consists of a length of 1.5mm thick walled silicone tubing which is fed through the eye of the bomb swivel. The lead is pushed about 3.75mm ($^3$/$_8$in) along the tubing as shown. The main line is threaded through the tube and the stop swivel attached. The end of the tube can be pushed over the stop swivel or the rig left free running.

Use these semi-fixed set-ups in preference to hanging the lead from the eye of the stop swivel. If the bomb is hung from the swivel and the line is broken above the lead then you will condemn a carp to towing a fixed lead about for several days.

## Stringer systems

The use of stringers has now become a standard part of winter and long-range carping. It is the most accurate method of placing free offerings with pinpoint accuracy around the hookbait and involves the use of polyvinyl alcohol (PVA) string or thread which dissolves in water. String does not dissolve as quickly as thread but is stronger if used straight from the packet and not separated into thinner strands.

The chief use for string is long distance fishing in summer with as many as six baits

**Far left:** PVA stringer tied to the bottom eye of the stop swivel.

**Left:** Exploding stringer with boilies trapped under tension against a fragment of Alka Seltzer tablet.

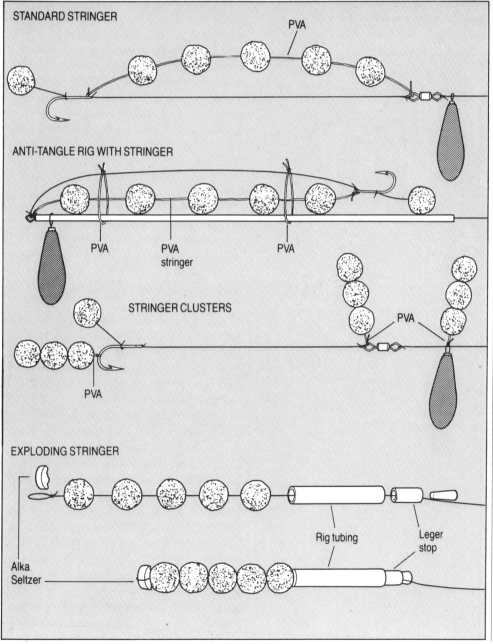

STANDARD STRINGER

PVA

ANTI-TANGLE RIG WITH STRINGER

PVA    PVA
stringer    PVA

STRINGER CLUSTERS

PVA

PVA

EXPLODING STRINGER

Rig tubing    Leger stop

Alka Seltzer

on one stringer. The boilies are threaded on a length of PVA string slightly longer than the hooklink and at roughly equal distances apart. One end of the PVA is then tied to the stop swivel and the other fastened to the hook. If used with anti-tangle tubing, the whole lot can be folded back and strapped to the tubing with two shorter pieces of PVA thread for stability in long-range casting.

PVA thread is more suitable for winter fishing. It dissolves very quickly and can be used in much the same way as string or to carry the baits in small clusters on the lead, stop swivel or hook.

Another technique that has earned extra fish in recent seasons is my own exploding stringer system. It incorporates a short length of anti-tangle tubing, leger stop, fragment of Alka Seltzer tablet and some boilies.

To set the rig up, make a small hole in the free offerings with a large baiting needle or one-eighth drill. Tie a small loop in one end of the pole elastic then break off a piece of Alka Seltzer tablet and insert it in the loop. Feed the drilled boilies down the elastic and slide on a short piece of anti-tangle tube. The length of the tube is governed by the final length of un-stretched elastic. Finally, stretch out the elastic to its full extent and lock everything in position under tension with the leger stop. The exploding stringer is then ready to be attached to the stop swivel. After casting out, the Alka Seltzer tablet dissolves in about 45 seconds and the elastic retracts into the rig tubing leaving the boilies free. In practice, the elastic recoils with such force that it sends the boilies flying several inches apart.

## Jobs for a float

Carp anglers rarely tackle up with a float these days because it is not regarded as a mainstream method. But I seldom step on the bank without my two favourite float patterns; the Peter Drennan Loafer and Giant Crystal.

I use a single swanshot capacity Loafer for dropping the bait in tiny gaps among lily pads, in weed beds or through trailing branches. It is fished as a slider with the line passed through the bottom end only. Sufficient shot to cock the float are fixed about 4in from the hook and a Billy Lane sliding stop knot is tied on the line at the required depth. This is a very compact rig and casts neatly into tight corners or it can be inched back into position after deliberately overcasting.

The 3AAA Giant Crystal is used for stalking fish where there is more room for manoeuvre. Two locking shots fix the float at the appropriate depth and the remaining weights are bunched close to the hook if I'm looking for a lift bite or very early warning — for example, when particle fishing. The shots are spaced out in descending size towards the hook if it

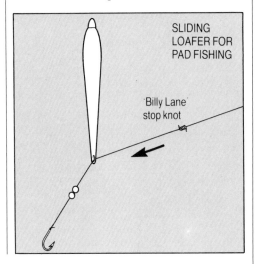

SLIDING LOAFER FOR PAD FISHING

'Billy Lane' stop knot

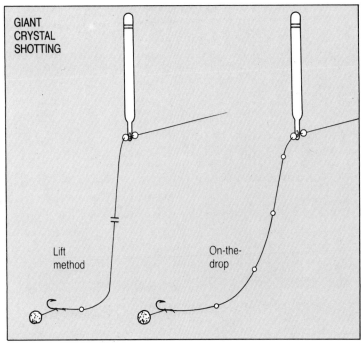

GIANT CRYSTAL SHOTTING

Lift method

On-the-drop

appears the bait needs presenting on-the-drop style. These floats might seem heavy for the job but remember they will probably be fished on 15lb line in snaggy swims. Use anything smaller and the rig will be totally unbalanced.

# Fishing over silt

The worst silt problem I have ever experienced was on a shallow lake where long distance casting sunk a 2oz lead as much as 45cm (18in) into the soft bottom. If you fished a 30cm (12in) hooklink on that lake the bait vanished from view. There are several ways of overcoming this.

## Depth of silt

The first job is to discover just how deep the lead is burying in the silt. You can quickly take a precise measurement by securing a bomb to the end of the main line and then running a 2m (6ft) length of white wool from the lead swivel back up the line and tying it off. The bomb is cast out and quickly retrieved with the rod held high all the time. What happens is that the bomb drags the white wool down into the silt and you can judge the depth by the length of wool that's discoloured by the silt. The dirty length of wool will

be slightly deeper than the layer of silt penetrated by the bomb because of the angle of retrieve, which is to your advantage when assembling the rig.

## Paternoster rig

Make up a running paternoster rig starting with a lead link that is approximately 30cm (12in) longer than the depth of the silt. Attach the lead at one end and the running swivel at the other. Slip this swivel on the main line and then attach a stop swivel followed by the hook length which should be roughly one third of the bomb link. For example, a 90cm (36in) bomb link equals a 30cm (12in) hooklink. Experience has shown this to be the most tangle-free ratio.

The rig can also be fished fixed but if that is your choice use the same breaking strain line for both main line and hook length with a weaker bomb link. That way the bomb link breaks first if you get snagged solid. The same dimensions can be used with a Drennan welded ring or swivel at the junction of main line and bomb link. If you're using a swivel, attach the hooklink on the bottom eye. Nylon hooklinks are preferred with this rig but anti-tangle tubing can be fixed above the bomb swivel with a soft Dacron bottom.

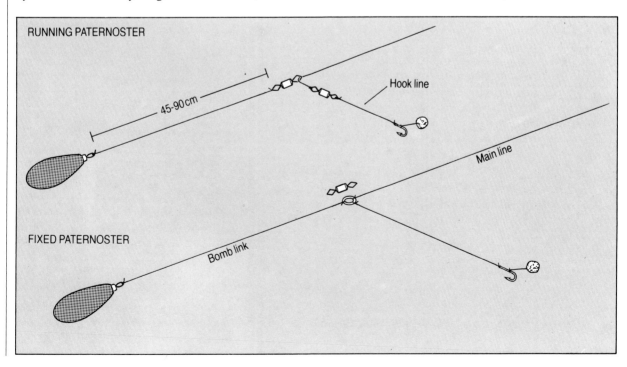

RUNNING PATERNOSTER

45-90 cm

Hook line

Main line

FIXED PATERNOSTER

Bomb link

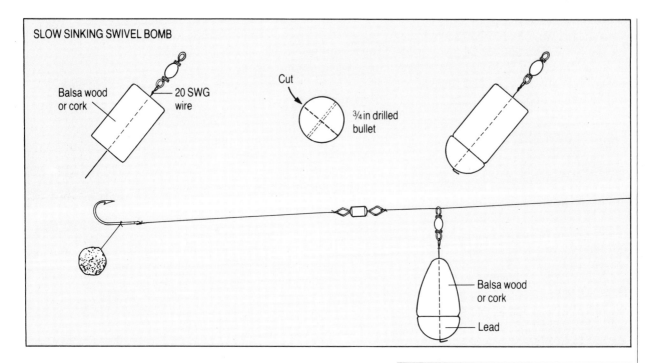

SLOW SINKING SWIVEL BOMB

Balsa wood or cork

20 SWG wire

Cut

¾ in drilled bullet

Balsa wood or cork

Lead

### Slow sinking bomb

If you're fishing over silt at short range or if you don't need a tight line to overcome drag, then a slow sinking bomb is the solution. They are not manufactured commercially so you'll have to make your own.

The first step is to feed a short length of 20 SWG brass or stainless steel wire through the eye of a swivel and twist it back on itself two or three times. Then take a 3cm (1.25in) length of balsa dowel or cork of about 2cm (¾in) diameter and push the wire through the centre of it. Cut a ¾in diameter drilled bullet lead in half across the section of the hole. Slide it up the wire cut side first, bend over the end of wire and trim off. Sand down the balsa or cork body into a pear-shape and drop the bomb into a tin of varnish for a waterproof seal. The slow sinking bomb can be fished on a conventional rig and will rest on the silt or sink very slightly into it.

### Disc bomb

This is a medium range rig for silt bottoms incorporating a plastic disc with a hole in the centre which is snapped over the swivel of the bomb. The diameter of the disc is dictated by the weight of the bomb.

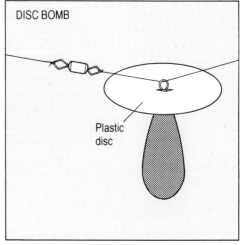

DISC BOMB

Plastic disc

For a 2oz lead you'll need a 2in disc and so on. The bomb is again fished on a normal rig and when cast out the disc steadies the fall of the bomb through the water resulting in a soft landing on the silt. The advantage of this rig is that it can be fished on a relatively tight line and is not so affected by drift and drag.

### Bait for silt

All the rigs suggested for silty bottoms should be used with a fairly light bait or one with a large, flat surface. Flat-sided particles such as kidney beans are better

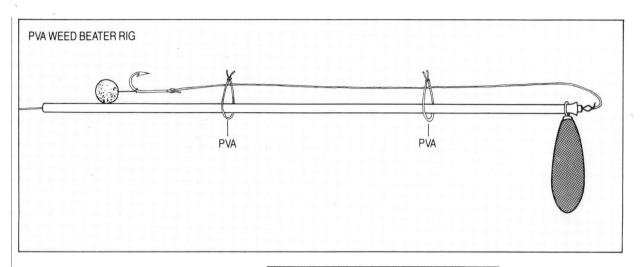

PVA WEED BEATER RIG

PVA          PVA

than maples. If you prepare your own boilies they are better flattened before boiling to make them penny-shaped. This will stop them sinking into the silt. If you are fishing at long range and round boilies are preferred then a pop-up would be an advantage.

## Fishing in weed

A swim choked with weed seems to frighten the life out of most anglers, but the underwater jungle is not half as bad as it seems. Rooted water-plants are often no different in construction from any other type of plant. Most tend to be thin with straightish stems fanning out into large dense heads. Weed viewed from the surface might appear tight packed but down on the bottom the stems are often several feet apart. Blanket or silt weed is rather different in make-up as it is un-rooted and its thickness and position changes daily depending on weather conditions.

Rooted weed is the easier of the two to tackle. It is chiefly a question of penetrating the surface canopy to reach the less dense area below. One answer is a Dacron anti-tangle rig with the hooklink strapped along the tubing at two or three points using PVA thread. The lead forces the surface fronds of weed apart, allowing the PVA parcelled rig to brush through without getting snagged up. The PVA melts leaving the baits presented among the roots. It is important not to attempt to

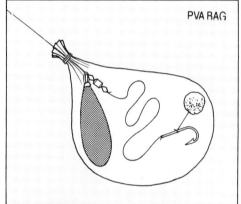

PVA BAG

**Below:** Green floating putty moulded around a short length of rig tubing makes a good controller in heavily weeded swims. You'll find it doesn't snag as readily when inching it back through pads to position the bait.

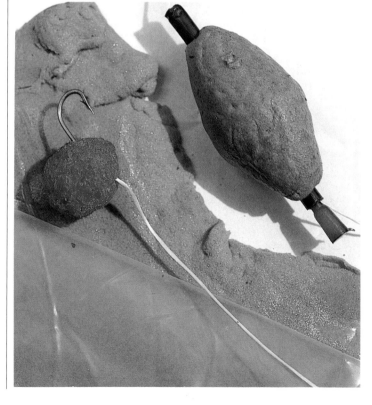

move the rig after casting because the main line will immediately foul the surface canopy.

If the surface weed is too dense for this rig then the ultimate solution is a PVA bag with the hooklink, bait and lead neatly folded up inside. Tie the bag off around the main line so nothing is left exposed. Ideally, the bag should crash down vertically through the water. It's possible to flip the bag 6m (20ft) up in the air even when fishing at comparatively short range but the lead must not be moved after the rig has come to rest.

### Blanket-weed rigs

Presenting a bait over blanket weed can be done on a paternoster type rig with a pop-up or flat-sided bait. If the carp are cruising just above the layers of weed use a pop-up on a 22cm (9in) hooklink. The length of the bomb link is determined by the weed layers.

This rig can also be fished with a flat-sided bait, such as sweetcorn, which stands out clearly on blanket weed. Carp love mooching up and down sucking off food and when they are feeding in this manner try a paternoster with a 30cm (12in) hooklink. As before, the length of the bomb link is decided by the depth of weed and it should be weaker than the main line or hooklink. Both recommended rigs for swims containing blanket weed must be fished with tight lines to ensure the bait is correctly positioned.

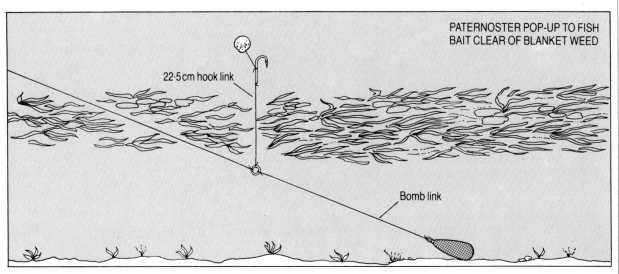

PATERNOSTER POP-UP TO FISH BAIT CLEAR OF BLANKET WEED

22·5 cm hook link

Bomb link

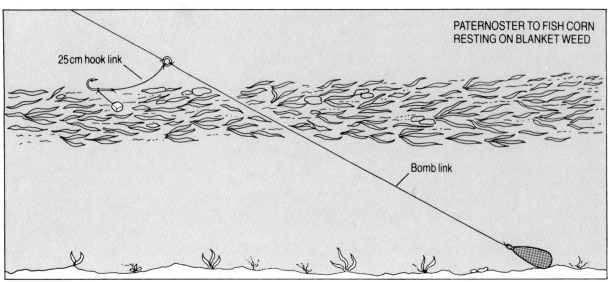

PATERNOSTER TO FISH CORN RESTING ON BLANKET WEED

25 cm hook link

Bomb link

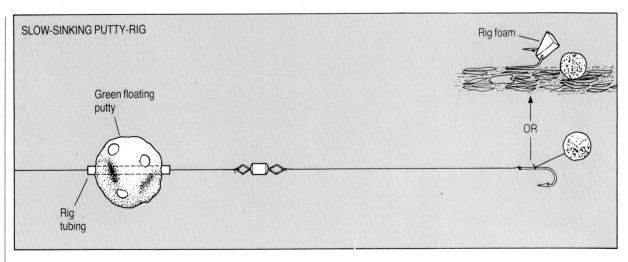

SLOW-SINKING PUTTY-RIG

Rig foam

Green floating putty

Rig tubing

OR

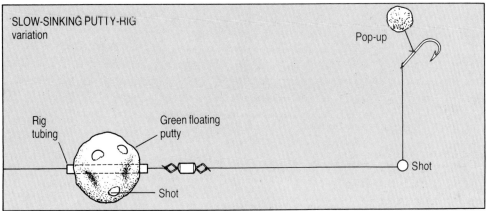

SLOW-SINKING PUTTY-RIG
variation

Pop-up

Rig tubing

Green floating putty

Shot

Shot

On waters where carp will not tolerate tight lines, I switch to a very slow sinking rig constructed with floating green putty. Rig tubing comes in handy yet again. This time you will require a short length of 2mm diameter. Mould the putty around the outside leaving about an eighth of an inch of exposed tubing at each end. Then push some split-shot into the putty until it just about sinks. The length of tubing and quantity of putty depends on the distance you need to cast. The main line is threaded through the tubing and a stop swivel attached followed by the hooklink. If fishing at short range you can use a silicone rubber as a stop with a piece of cocktail stick inserted.

Where the blanket weed is exceptionally wispy and the hook is continually masked then it needs suspending with a piece of rig foam on the bend. A similar method can be used with pop-up boilies when fishing for carp that are cruising just above the blanket weed.

## Pick of the bottom baits

Tinned meats, paste baits and boilies are the leading bottom baits. Pork luncheon meat and Bacon Grill are the favourite meats. The rule with pastes is the stronger the better. Gorgonzola and Danish Blue stand out and the best meat pastes are luncheon meat, liver and beef. Dog-food and cat-food pastes remain good standbys but I prefer fish pastes: sardine, pilchard, squid and anchovy seem most potent. Boilies divide into four groups: fish, meat, birdseed and milk protein mixes. If you are adding your own flavours the most consistent catchers are maple, cream, strawberry, blueberry, caramel, malt, liquorice, clove, bun spice, sweetcorn, black cherry, peanuts, mivi, salmon, shrimp, anchovy, blue cheese and honey. Use them alone or blended together. Favourite shelf-life boilies include dairy cream fudge and king prawn.

# BITE INDICATION

Most carp anglers persevere with the leger for the lion's share of their fishing and that has produced tremendous improvements in bite indication systems to help relay the merest flicker of interest in the unseen bait.

## Development of indicators

Today's sophisticated electronic alarms and problem-free indicators are a far cry from the era of dough bobbins and silver paper cylinders blowing in the wind and creating horrendous birdsnests. Looking back, it is fascinating to recall how we arrived at the modern self-hooking rigs and highly versatile indicators.

### Twitch bites

Much of the stimulus for improved designs came about because of unhittable twitch bites. Before the hair rig emerged, carp which had been caught many times often rejected a suspicious looking bait, giving a short, sharp lift on the indicator and no more. That became known as a twitch. It occurred because the fish felt something was wrong with the bait and was able to blow it out with such force that an inch or two of line was jerked through the bomb swivel. The indicator was momentarily jerked upwards as a result. This frustrating performance could be repeated several times in as many minutes.

Hitting these lightning fast twitch bites became something of a challenge. For several years, everybody used Fairy Liquid bottle tops as indicators, hanging them on the line between the butt and second ring. But it was hit-and-miss stuff.

### Sizzling runs

The breakthrough in bite indication systems really had to wait until the invention of self-hooking rigs. As soon as bold, fast runs on the hair rig became routine then swinging bottle-tops were made obsolete. Fishing with an open bale arm was clearly necessary faced with sizzling runs instead of hesitant twitches and that coincided with the birth of the monkey climber. Plastic indicators sliding on steel needles and buzzer bars are now the nation's choice — and they've improved our efficiency by 101 per cent.

Starting at ground level and working up, here are my recommendations for the chief component parts of the modern rod support, indicator and alarm system.

## Bank sticks

The choice in bank sticks is between cheap, aluminium ones which need replacing several times during the course of a season or those made in stainless steel or heavy aero-aluminium which should last for years. Ultimately, you'll find lightweight aluminium sticks which buckle first time out a poor investment. They're just not sturdy enough to be hammered into hard ground.

So choose a stainless-steel model with an extending inner rod for height adjustment. Check that the adjusting thumbscrew is large enough to lock up the inner stick securely. Some thumbscrews are too

Adjustable bank sticks should feature a large thumbscrew.

small and with cold fingers you'll never get sufficient purchase to tighten them down. It follows that the inner rod should slide freely with no signs of corrosion which could cause it to jam against the outer sleeve. The standard three-eighths BSF thread on the bank stick will take a lot of punishment and must be made of stainless steel or brass and not aluminium which corrodes too quickly.

## Buzzer bars

A buzzer bar is screwed on and off the bank stick repeatedly through the season in all kinds of weather. Again, the only choice of material for strength and reliability is stainless steel.

Let's look at a simple two rod assembly. I prefer to position both rods at the same height above the ground with the rear buzzer bar narrower than the front. That makes it possible to fish a much straighter line towards the leads assuming the hookbaits will mostly be just a few yards apart.

The rear buzzer bar is fitted with high sided, cupped rod-rest heads. Screw-in types are all right but for my money you can't beat the push-on, flexible rod-rest

heads. These slide over brass studs screwed into the female threads on the bar. Whichever type you choose, the rod butt must sit snugly within the rest so it cannot be knocked off. An advantage with the stud and push-on fitting is that it's much easier to line up the rod. With a screw-in design there's always the worry that the thread might bottom out leaving the rod-rest head at the wrong angle.

The front buzzer bar takes the electronic alarms or V-shaped rod-rests with a central channel which allows the line to flow freely. Where the terrain is too soft for a bank stick to hold steady, use a stabiliser. This twin-spiked accessory locks on the bank stick giving the same sort of grip as though you were forcing the prongs of a garden fork deep in the ground. With a buzzer bar carrying two rods it's only necessary to stabilise the rear bank stick as the weight of the rods will do the rest.

My custom-made buzzer bars are capable of taking two or three rods. The span is adjustable, making it very versatile. The centre position is fixed directly above the bank stick and the outer ones are adjustable on a keyed slide — a simple push and fit manoeuvre. The bank sticks holding the buzzer bars are staked about 60cm (2ft) apart with the reels positioned just inside the rear rod-rest heads leaving most of the butt sections overhanging.

## Monkey climbers

Kent angler Ricky Gibbinson takes the credit for developing the original monkey climber. His indicator was a flimsy tube of white plastic sheet with a hole cut out for the line. It was placed on an upright needle directly below the rod and just in front of the spool and worked a treat. The only drawback was that once you had picked up the rod and closed the bale arm, the indicator was no longer trapped on the needle and was easily blown away. Now needles have a stop at the top to prevent this happening and most indicators are machined from lightweight solid plastic with a wire clip-line retainer.

Choose your monkey climber with care because there are some diabolical models

**Above left:** Front buzzer bar with rod-rest heads fitted instead of alarms.

**Above:** Andy's push-on heads and high quality, stainless steel bar.

**Left:** The ideal set-up with stabiliser on the rear bank stick to hold everything rock steady.

on the market! The needle must be made from quality stainless steel that won't rust. The tip is normally flattened to prevent the indicator flying off but feel for any jagged edges which will be lethal on line. The same applies with monkey bodies — some injection moulded models are left with small burrs where they have been ejected from the press. Among the best commercially-made indicators is the Grease Monkey. It has a stainless steel needle coated with black PTFE to reduce friction and special care is taken to ensure there are no dangerous ragged edges. The body of the indicator is moulded in three take-apart sections which allows for

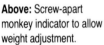

**Above:** Screw-apart monkey indicator to allow weight adjustment.

**A.** Greased monkey with snap-apart indicator. Probably the best buy among commercially-made indicators.
**B.** Flip-top monkey body moulded from PTFE with isotope chamber.

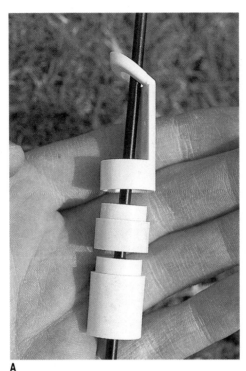

**A**

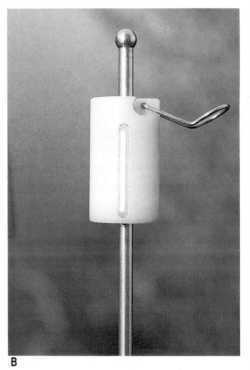

**B**

weight adjustment to suit conditions.

Most indicators are sold with a fixed line clip but the flip-top type of monkey body is better. On reaching the top of the needle, the retaining wire clip falls back completely free of the line, eliminating any possibility of snagging. I've had my flip-top indicators machined from solid PTFE which is superior to flimsy plastic and they're hollowed out with a screw-on bottom so I can insert different size weights. A waterproof magnet is moulded into the bottom which clasps the base of the steel needle with sufficient strength to combat undertow and drag. That effectively replaces a front line clip on the rod.

One final design feature on my flip-tops is a channel to slot in an isotope. It lights up the chamber of the indicator superbly at night.

## Setting up a monkey climber

The most direct way of setting up a monkey climb system is to push the needles straight into the ground just below the rod, either between the first and second ring or a couple of inches in front of the reel. But this is asking for trouble. Needles are soon damaged on gravel banks and there's always a temptation to bend them so that they line up correctly with the rod. After a few sessions of that sort of treatment the needles will look more like corkscrews.

By far the best method is to lift the needles clear of the ground by screwing them on a supporting bar which is firmly pegged in place with one or two spikes. Alternatively, fit an adjustable 'T' bar to the front or rear bank stick which again has lockable needle holding devices. The beauty of this is that once the bank sticks are securely positioned nothing else has to be driven into the ground.

Remember that monkey climb systems are not maintenance free. It is essential

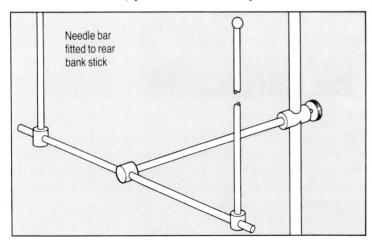

Needle bar fitted to rear bank stick

to keep the needles spotlessly clean. A fleck of grit splashed up by rain could find its way between the needle and the bore of the monkey body resulting in seizure. And that's potentially devastating. I have seen a complete monkey assembly ripped out of the ground by a runaway carp and the line eventually snapped where the indicator had jammed solid on the needle. There are a couple of ways to avoid this happening. One is to lay out a rod mat on the ground through which the bank sticks and needle bars are inserted. That will give complete protection against splashing even in the heaviest downpour. The other option is to set the needle bar higher than normal putting it beyond the reach of spray.

## Line clips

Front and back line clips are small items but they're of major importance. Shop-bought plastic clips snap neatly around the rod but you can easily make your own from slithers of carbon with the edges smoothed down.

Clipping down, this is how you'd set the indicators when fishing the rods high over weed or with a free-running bolt rig. It's also the system for strong winds and undertow. The line is held in the front clip only (INSET).

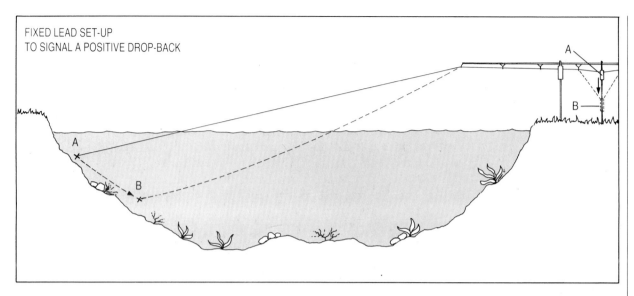

FIXED LEAD SET-UP
TO SIGNAL A POSITIVE DROP-BACK

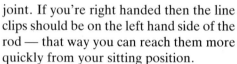

**Below:** Clipping up...the correct way when fast runs are expected on bolt type rigs incorporating a fixed lead.

The butt clip goes immediately above the spool of the reel and is strapped in place with electrical tape. Secure the front clip between the first and second intermediates down from the tip ring on the top joint. If you're right handed then the line clips should be on the left hand side of the rod — that way you can reach them more quickly from your sitting position.

The front clip serves as a wind and drift beater with a free-running rig. Clip up with minimum tension to overcome the conditions and set the monkey climb at the base of the needle. I don't recommend front clipping with a bolt rig because a vicious take smashes the monkey body into the rod and can damage it.

Bolt rigs should be firmly back clipped to create resistance and help set the hook. In this case, the needle is normally fished just in front of an open spool with the monkey climb up high. When a carp belts off with the bait, the line bursts from the clip and the monkey body drops an inch or two on the needle before hovering on the spot as line continues to peel from the spool at a furious rate.

The same approach is also adopted with a fixed lead, especially when fishing against an island or the far bank. At these times, the carp usually run towards you, slackening the line between the lead and rod tip. With a front clip you'd get no indication at all from the angler's side of the rod tip unless you were lucky enough to spot the line go slack. But with a back clip and the monkey at the top of the needle, there's a very positive drop-back. Add as much weight as possible to the monkey body to provide the earliest possible indication.

## Butt foam

When it's necessary to keep as much line as possible off the water to prevent it scraping a gravel bar or snagging a weed bed, then a wad of foam stuck in the first or second ring of the rod will do the job. It maintains constant tension on the line raising it above the obstruction even after a run has developed.

Another time to use foam is when strong winds create heavy undertow. Line tends to belly out in undertow as a hard running fish pours line from the spool and the time taken to wind down and make contact is prolonged. That could be time enough for the loose line to foul a snag in the swim. Foam solves the problem by maintaining direct contact with the fish at all times.

Many anglers are also great believers in foam for bolt rigs. They reckon the even build-up of resistance through the foam is a more efficient way of pulling the hook into the carp's mouth than the customary bolt rig method of back clipping very tightly. When line is suddenly jerked from a very tight clip and then falls limp, it could catapult the lead and result in a lightly pricked hook bouncing free.

Well, that's the theory — only experience will determine the right method for you. When using butt foam, trap the line against the bottom of the rod ring and not at the side or top. If the line is pressed against the top of the ring it could get damaged as it digs into the foam under the pressure of a hooked fish.

Top of the range Super Compact Optonics fitted with ears to hold the rods steady in very windy weather.

## Electronic bite alarms

Staring at a static monkey climb all day strains the eyes and makes it impossible to scan the lake effectively for signs of fish activity. A reliable electronic bite alarm permits you to keep your eyes peeled and get on with other things such as baiting up and rig tying without any fear of missing a take. For long sessions, they're an absolute must. But don't fall into the trap of thinking that electronic alarms give the freedom to wander down the bank for a chat with a mate. The No.1 rule in carp fishing is never to leave rods unattended.

### Antenna alarms and Optonics

The most basic alarm is the antenna type where the line is drawn around an upright arm. Once it tightens as a result of a run, a pair of contacts are drawn together completing the circuit and sounding the alarm. These alarms can be adjusted to register a slight increase in pressure on the line but they will not react to a loosening of the line.

The best-selling indicator is undoubtedly the Optonic with its rotating vane wheel on which the line rests. Any movement of the line spins the wheel and cuts through a photo-electric cell giving off a bleep.

The top of the range Optonic has adjustable tone and volume with two light emitting diodes (LED's). One LED glows all

**Left:** Plug of foam to prevent false indication in adverse weather.

the time the vane wheel is turning and the circuit is being broken. The other LED is latching and regardless of whether or not the run is continuing it will stay alight for several seconds. This is a great help when fishing multiple rods. A slight pucker of the line signalling a twitch or line bite is often encouraging news and it's good to know on which rod it occurred.

The Optonic bleeps whichever direction the vane wheel rotates and responds immediately to drop-back bites, unlike antenna alarms. But the roles are reversed when the only indication you get is a slow tightening between lead and rod tip with no actual line taken. The Optonic would not register this kind of take but the antenna alarm can do so.

## Strike at a nodding rod tip

It's impossible to legislate for every kind of take. For instance, there'll be times when the bites are very indecisive no matter what kind of line clip and rig you're using. These nudges at the bait might only show up as a slight nod of the rod tip. But strange to report, if you time the strike correctly the finicky fish are often very easily hooked! I recall one memorable winter session fishing at long range when I had no firm runs but finished with a dozen good fish on the bank. I struck every time the rod tip nodded. Other anglers on the lake waited for fast takes to develop and blanked.

### Tap bites at night

Spotting slight pulls in daylight is no problem but at night it becomes impossible without repositioning the Optonic so that it is raised up and fished in front of the rod with the line running over it and then through to the bomb. Sounds awkward but it works! You'll need an extra bank stick and buzzer bar to place the Optonic about 30cm (12in) in front of the rod tip and about 15cm (6in) higher. After casting out, tighten down to the lead so the rod tip is under tension and pointing upwards. Any slight up or down movement of the tip will register on the Optonic.

## Preparing for every run

The power and speed of a run clearly depend on the rig and distance being fished. These factors determine how the indication system is pre-set and it's important to get it right otherwise good chances may go begging. First, here are summaries of my three main lines of attack depending on distance.

### Margin fishing

This calls for an open bale arm approach because carp hooked in the margins will make a blistering run. Fishing with a closed bale is simply asking for trouble. Front clips are unnecessary because undertow shouldn't have much of an effect. There is also little point in fishing the

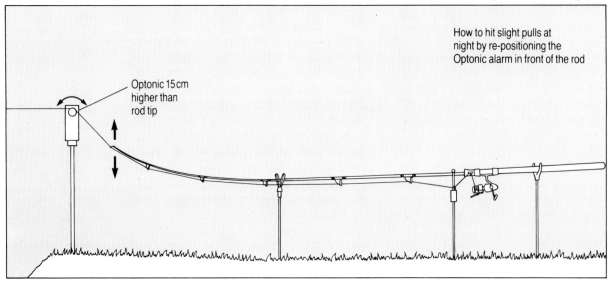

How to hit slight pulls at night by re-positioning the Optonic alarm in front of the rod

Optonic 15cm higher than rod tip

monkey climb at the top of the needle in anticipation of a drop-back as fish are unlikely to charge straight at the bank. A tight line between rod tip and lead would also spook them.

The first move is to position the rods low to the ground with just the tips projecting over the water's edge. Leave a fair amount of slack line in front of the rod and do not clip up in any way. Select the lightest monkey climb body and locate the needle a couple of inches in front of the open spool.

## Medium range fishing

At medium range in open water the approach is similar to that for the margins except that the rods are slightly higher and they need to overhang the water as much as possible. Clip up if there's any undertow or with a fixed lead. Fishing at this range, fast takes are still possible and providing there's no immediate danger from snags then an open bale arm is favourite.

The speed of the take will be much reduced when fishing tight up against an island or the far bank. The carp will move right, left, or straight towards your own bank and that means back clipping with the indicator perched at the top of the needle. Fishing the bale arm open or closed is a matter of personal preference in this situation.

## Extreme long range fishing

Beyond 100 yards I like to use a running lead rig. The fish could move off in any direction and line pulled through a stationary bomb is easily recognisable. When forced to fish a fixed lead at extreme range I select the heaviest monkey body in my box and will even add extra weight in bad weather. With so much line out, a carp can tow a bomb quite some distance before registering an indication at the rod. If you fish a lightweight monkey climb, that carp could be in the margins before you realise what's going on! Point the rods as far out over the water as possible and directly at the leads. If a shallow bar intervenes, fish the rod tips much higher than the butts — it's not unusual to elevate the tips by as much as 5ft above the ground.

Also, don't forget that butt foam is well worth considering.

## Reel churner fishing

The three methods of attack described above allow you to sit back at your leisure. But at other times you'll need to hover over the rods ready for a quick strike followed by a rapid wind-down to stop a fish ploughing into trailing branches or other obstructions. So position the rods at a comfortable height for an instant strike. Fish with a closed bale arm and keep the line as taut as possible but without clipping up as this might spook the fish more than is necessary. Try to avoid a fixed lead for the same reason. Position the needle a couple of inches behind the Optonic so there's a fair distance between the reel and the monkey climb. This is an important point because a run will probably spin the reel round a couple of times before you've had a chance to grab the rod. The oscillating movement of the line just in front of the reel would certainly jam a monkey climb if it was fished tight up to a closed bale.

This type of set-up is often described as reel churner fishing. Reacting to a run is simply a matter of picking up the rod with one hand, grabbing the spinning reel-handle with the other and holding the carp on a tight line as hard as possible to prevent it reaching the danger area.

## Jungle stalking

There's another form of snag fishing, which demands a totally different approach to the reel churners, and that's hunting in the jungle for carp that will probably be feeding right under your feet. These overgrown sanctuaries are frequently the carp's preferred feeding grounds where they feel completely safe from angler pressure. The snags lie right around your bait and the aim is to give no line at all to the fish. It's heart-stopping action and the only way of tackling it is to hold the rod with a white plastic cylinder indicator hung on the line between the first and second rings. Kneel down and trap the rod between your thigh and elbow for stability.

## How hard should you strike?

Whack into a carp fleeing from the margins and the end result is likely to be a snapped line and lost fish. Instead of slamming into a fish at close quarters, close the bale arm and let it run off against a correctly pre-set clutch. Striking carp at medium range is less of a problem. There's a fair amount of room for error and an over enthusiastic strike will not normally do any harm. Fishing an open bale arm at medium range with no imminent danger from snags, close the bale and strike firmly while continually winding. If carried out correctly, you will feel a solid thump at the end of the rod as it comes to an abrupt stop when the hook is driven home. After conduct-

Andy feels a carp kick at long range as he winds down quickly to keep in touch.

ing many experiments with striking at fish at distances over 100 metres, I know it is a total waste of time. A powerful strike will barely move the bomb a couple of inches and that's not sufficient to drive a hook into a carp's mouth. It's far better to pick up the rod and wind down until you feel you can't retrieve any more line. Hold the rod as high as possible and pull it back over your shoulder maintaining a tight line. The fish will only be lightly pricked and the hook needs to be worked in deeper by constant pressure. Stalking fish at short range demands a firm strike. Make sure you are fishing with tackle equal to the punishment it will receive.

## Spotting the liners

Carp often bump into the line between the rod tip and lead resulting in false runs known as liners. It's more likely to happen in shallow water or over bars where the fish will be swimming very close to the lines for a great deal of the time. Distinguishing between a liner and the real thing is easy enough when you're not clipped up. The line normally catches on the fish's dorsal or tail fin for a second or two before falling free and the effect on the indicator is a slow rise followed by an equally steady descent to a point on the needle just short of its original position. If you're striking at what appear to be slow, confident takes and completely missing them, restrain yourself and wait to see if the indicator falls back. The chances are that you're striking in vain at liners. When fishing clipped up, it's much harder to detect a liner. Sometimes the line will immediately ping free, simply causing the rod tip to nod. But when the line is pulled clear of the clip the indicator will be sent flying up and down the needle several times under its own inertia. Delay the strike for a few seconds to check if the run develops properly — that's the only solution.

Never judge a carp's fighting qualities by its size alone. This modest mirror deceived Andy by demanding yards of line when first hooked over a shallow bar.

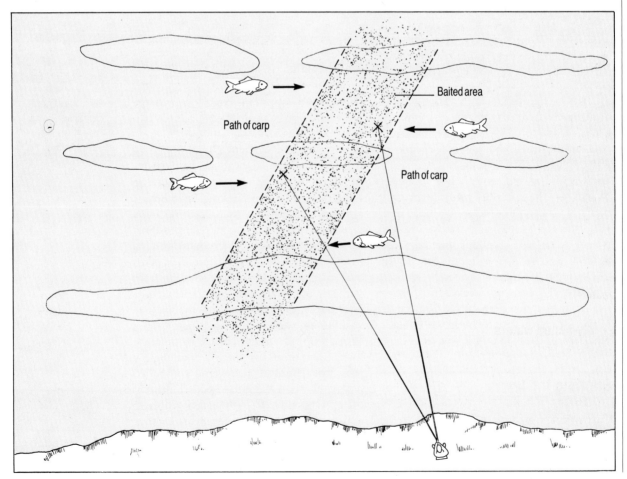

Baited area

Path of carp

Path of carp

Baited area

Path of carp

Path of carp

# TACKLE & TECHNIQUES

## Prebaiting principles

The need for a prebaiting programme largely depends on the amount of fishing which is being done on the water in question. Once this is known the correct technique for the type of water can be followed.

### Hard-fished waters

The carp in many lakes do not require any persuasion to show interest in hookbaits. This certainly applies on hard fished waters where baits are going in constantly and the fish instantly recognise coloured little balls as a food source. A prebaiting programme would not achieve anything on these carp circuit waters. All that's needed is to concentrate the loose feed during the session where it will be of greatest benefit.

For example, if a big shoal of feeding carp is likely to move through the swim there must be a large quantity of baits lying on the bottom to intercept and hold them. But where just the odd fish are patrolling then a handful of baits is adequate.

### Lightly-fished waters

Prebaiting becomes essential for consistent results on waters which are only lightly fished. It should be carried out regularly and, if practical, on a daily basis. Start off by scattering free offerings as widely as possible because carp are great wanderers and you want to be certain that they'll bump into your bait. On a small

pool this obviously presents no problem but a large lake will have to be divided up into smaller sections with each zone prebaited in rotation.

Introduce free offerings from 1m to 3m (3 to 10ft) apart on small waters, extending this to between 6 and 9m (20 and 30ft) on big lakes. Steadily build up on the amount going in rather than piling in thousands right at the outset on a virgin water. If baits are left uneaten for days they could go off and repel the carp and the process would have to be repeated from scratch.

Prebait lightly at first and gradually increase the quantity as the carp become familiar with the offerings. After a week or two of prebaiting the whole area, narrow it down to selected spots. Even on small waters it's a good plan to bait up about a dozen different swims to increase the options.

Finally, don't let up once you start catching carp. If there are only one or two anglers on the water, prebaiting must continue to prevent the fish losing interest.

**Opposite top:**
Diagonal spread of free offerings gives best chance of intercepting a fish.

**Opposite bottom:**
Cover move than one trough between bars on gravel pits to increase your options.

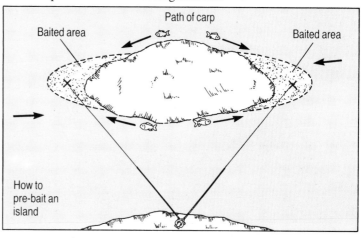

How to pre-bait an island

Particles pouch (top) and boilie cup fitted to catapults in the Drennan range.

### Points of interception

On a featureless water it is difficult to pinpoint the precise point at which carp will enter the swim but bait up in a diagonal pattern and your chances of intercepting patrolling fish are dramatically increased. The same method works well on gravel pits where carp follow the troughs between bars, usually sticking to one side rather than ploughing through the centre. Try to cover three bars if possible.

When fishing across to an island, bait each end instead of the middle and you're more likely to intercept carp moving in

Wrist-grip catapult powers hard boilies beyond 100 yards.

and out. Finally, if you're tackling a known hotspot it is just a matter of concentrating the free offering as tightly as possible around the hookbaits. When the hotspot lies beneath overhanging bushes, lay a trail of boilies leading out to the hookbait. Carp approach these snaggy areas by well-defined routes and it makes sense to bait around the entrance and exit.

## Feeding accessories

Firing out free offerings of bait presents no problem if you select the right catapult or other accessory.

### Catapults

There isn't a catapult made that will deal with all baiting tasks. For single boilies, cubes of luncheon meat and anything similar, a small pouch offers more firepower. Spraying particles or catapulting several boilies simultaneously, calls for a larger pouch. The quality of the latex elastics is the key to performance and with heavy use these might require replacement two or three times a season. Standard catapults are good for baiting swims within medium range — say 50 metres.

Baiting up with large boilies at extreme range is a job for the Marksman hunting catapult which is used in the United States to kill small game. A sturdy steel frame, wrist support and very powerful latex elastics make it possible to fire single baits in excess of 100 yards.

### Throwing stick

A throwing stick is the best tool for hurling hard, small diameter boilies up to 80 yards. It's surprising how quickly you can distribute several hundred boilies with a well designed model such as the swan-necked Cobra. Baits leave the throwing stick at great speed and they'll travel furthest when skimmed just above the surface. In fact, it's not unusual to see a bait fly inches above the water and then suddenly lift before splashdown. Up to about 65 metres range, three or four baits can be fired at the same time.

## Bait dropper

Feeding particles at distances beyond about 50 yards is way beyond the capacity of a standard catapult. This is a job for the bait dropper. I've found Gardner Tackle's Bait Rocket ideal for slinging out a handful of particles or mini boilies beyond 60 metres. The dropper is cast out on a beefy rod with a test curve of around 2.5lb and on hitting the water it turns turtle, spilling out the particles. Incidentally, use a 15lb shock leader with the dropper to avoid a potentially dangerous crack-off.

## Mixer Fixer

Another useful baiting aid is the Mixer Fixer. This is a combined controller and floating bait dispenser. The baits are fed into a cigar-shaped tube below a polyball sight bob which is clearly visible at long distance. A counterbalance weight ensures the Mixer Fixer cocks correctly in the water and as the polyball floats above the tube opening in its cradle, the floaters inside bob to the surface right round the hookbait. In favourable conditions, the Mixer Fixer can be cast 60 metres.

**Left:** Throwing stick.

**Below left:** Bait Rocket for up-ending particles in a distant swim.

**Below:** The Mixer Fixer with its polyball sight bob serves a dual purpose - it acts as a controller and bait distributor.

A softer actioned rod is needed for explosive action at close quarters with margin feeders.

## Life span of bait

Having carried out a prebaiting programme, what sort of life expectancy should you expect from any particular bait? Some seem to prosper season after season while others lose their potency after catching a few fish. The term 'blown bait' is often used to describe an offering that has lost its powers of attraction. In my experience this a rare occurrence.

Particles have a long life span and individual fish fall for the same type repeatedly. A carp must pick up many thousands of particles before coming across the hookbait and the ratio between the baits consumed and the number of times it is caught is obviously much lower than with boilies. A carp may only have to eat 50 boilies before chewing on a hook, therefore it will become wary of the boilie much more quickly. Certainly it's true to say that individual carp are captured fewer times on a specific flavour of boilie compared with a single type of particle.

The more subtle the flavour, the longer the life span of the bait. That's the unwritten rule.

## Margin tackle

Now to the choice of tackle, starting with that for margin and mid-range fishing.

### Rod and reel

The right rod for margin to mid-range fishing is a through-action 12ft model made of carbon or a Kevlar mix with a test curve between $1\frac{1}{2}$ and 2lb. There are many excellent blanks on the market and the development of lightweight reel fittings and friction-free rings makes these softer rods a pleasure to fish.

Carp hooked at close range put the whole tackle under tremendous stress. The rod must be capable of tolerating the first surge of power from the fish and through-action is the only choice. A fast taper casting tool would be more of a barrier than a buffer in this situation, leading to excessive strain on the line.

As most margin to mid-range work demands an open bale arm, my choice of reel is an Abu Cardinal 55 fixed spool. These reels offer a superbly reliable bale arm mechanism which closes at the first time of asking. The clutch at the rear is very positive and won't seize up at critical moments. A smoothly operating roller completes a fine reel.

### Line and hook

It follows from the above that the line needs to possess plenty of stretch. So make sure you steer clear of the low diameter, pre-stretched nylons which would be too unforgiving. Reliable brands include Maxima and Sylcast but do not use a breaking strain of less than 8lb.

Finally to the choice of hook. The best pattern is a forged, round or crystal bend, medium shanked model. Most hooks are mass-produced and even the top brands vary from batch to batch, especially as a result of differences which occur in the hardening and tempering process. Test every hook before tying it on and reject those which bend out of shape at the slightest pressure. A highly recommended pattern is the Drennan Super Specialist which is extremely tough and chemically sharpened. The neat small barb is perfect to assist self-pricking.

# Margin methods

For sheer excitement you can't beat margin fishing whether it's the dramatic heaving of a carp out of lily pads or the tense excitement of sitting quietly at night listening to the fish slurping among the reeds. But let's begin with bubbler fishing.

### Chasing bubblers

This is a strange game. There are times when virtually every bubbler I cast at produces a fish on the bank. At other times the baits are completely ignored for no apparent reason.

Tackle a bubbler by casting the hookbait a few feet in front of the anticipated path of the carp. Where it's difficult to cast accurately, intercept the fish by baiting up several yards in front of it with the hookbait left among the free offerings.

But before deciding on your approach, spend time observing the speed, direction and regularity of the bubbling. You must

Top performer. Strong points of the Cardinal 55 are its super bale arm system and efficient clutch.

be spot on with the cast because carp love feeding in a straight line and are unwilling to make detours.

It's often said that worms are essential for catching bubblers but that's simply not true. Provided the bait has a good track record on the water, the fish will pick it up. And they usually won't mind 2oz of lead plopping in when they're feeding in this manner.

If weather conditions or the distance at which the fish is feeding obstructs accurate casting, then place a tight group of free offerings along the anticipated route. You'll require about 50 boilies to distract the carp from its natural feed. Any less than 50 and the baits could be ignored; any more and it's unlikely a single carp will clear them all up.

Carp which bubble spasmodically are easier to catch, possibly because they are not totally preoccupied with the natural feed and are willing to try something different.

Again, there will be a pattern to the bubbling even when it's of short duration. The carp will tend to send up a trail of bubbles, perhaps for 3m (10ft) or so, then move along a similar distance before repeating the bubbling and usually head and shouldering on the surface in between. These carp move quite fast so to increase your chances of a successful interception cast two baits about 2 to 2.75m (6 to 8ft) apart in the next area where you calculate the fish will go down. If this fails after several attempts, catapult about 50 boilies right in its path.

A

**Double trouble in the weeds**

When the carp bury themselves among the weed stalks, there's always the risk of biting off more than you can chew. But Andy is more determined than most.
**A.** After catapulting Mixers across this clearing in the weeds all morning, Andy finally flicks his hookbait into the path of a common that he calculates has probably sucked down its own packet of free offerings! But the bend in the rod is not caused by the target 20-pounder...another fish nipped in first. Andy hasn't got a clue as to its size.
**B.** One sudden splash on the surface and then everything locks solid. Because he was taken unawares, Andy has got far more line out than he would like and the fish becomes well weeded.

The beauty of bubblers is that it won't take you long to find out if you've put the hookbait in the right place. You'll either get a take or see another burst of bubbles hit the surface just past the hookbaits.

## Fishing in lily pads

Before casting a bait among lily pads give some thought to how you're actually going to land a fish. A good casting position from behind a bush might be fine for concealment but it's useless if a carp rushes around the other side and prevents you applying maximum pressure to gain line. Move down the bank a few yards instead where it's possible to stand at the water's edge and net a fish.

There's little point in laying the landing net on the ground alongside the casting position if the fish must be brought to the bank somewhere else. The net should be correctly positioned before casting.

Extracting a carp from the centre of lily pads can be played in two distinct ways: by brute force or by stealth. The heavy-handed method is short lived but dramatic. The sequence is to strike, wind down and possibly step back a few paces — all in one movement — without giving

an inch of line. The carp is turned over on its back in a cascade of weed and water and bundled into the net before it realises what's happened. Any reduction of pressure is likely to end in disaster.

With the softly, softly approach, the carp is permitted its first powerful rush. This builds up weed on the line, exerting enough weight and pressure to bring the fish to a halt. The weed is certain to festoon the carp's head, masking its vision and forcing it to slow down. There'll be a few heavy lunges as it attempts to bury itself still further into the weed bed but now is the moment to gently increase the pressure, moving the rod from side to side. This sawing motion on the line should free some of the weed and when back in direct contact with the fish again its head is forced round at a different angle. That will provoke it to bolt in a different direction and the procedure is repeated. Eventually, the fish will run out of steam and you can coax it into the net.

If the carp gets stuck fast in the weed, then resort to hand lining which applies even greater pressure. Keep pulling the line from side to side and it should move off again.

B

C

**C.** Swinging the rod at different angles provokes the carp into burying itself even further into the weed. It looks a hopeless case.
**D.** With the water up to his chest, Andy probes with the net and gathers up the carp which is heavily festooned with smashed weed stalks.
**E.** Edging backwards towards the bank there's a realisation that the rest of the session will be spent in damp discomfort!
**F.** The cause of all the trouble - a double-figure mirror with a rudder for a tail.

D

E

The rough and tumble of pad fishing makes it imperative to fish as simple a terminal rig as possible — swivels and leger weights have a habit of catching up on lily roots.

Occasionally, you might decide to wade into the water to deal with a particularly difficult fish. It sounds daft but I have seen anglers do this and leave the rod and landing net on the bank! As soon as they near the carp it bolts off with renewed vigour leaving the unfortunate angler marooned. Far better to maintain constant pressure and gradually work your way towards the fish with rod and net, freeing the line as you go.

F

Loafer float rig for precision casting among the pads.

Never mind the distractions, keep the eyes peeled for signs of carp moving in over the baits at long range!

There's great satisfaction in spending a few hours creeping round the margins with a pocketful of baits and a float. For a great deal of the time you won't actually have a bait in the water. The priority is to plot the route of a patrolling fish and carefully present free offerings in its path. When its suspicions have been overcome, the floatfished bait can be gently lowered into position.

After spending some time observing fish in close-up, you should be capable of telling whether or not a carp is likely to take a bait by its body movements. At first, it will probably pass over the free offerings but if all is well it will start picking up the odd bait. The more it takes, the more confident it will become. Once it starts greedily rooting around in search of more bait, it's time to move in. But don't be in too much of a hurry. Drop in your hookbait when the carp is several feet away and resist the temptation to keep moving it if the fish doesn't show interest on the first pass.

On other occasions it might prove impossible to lure the carp into accepting bait. Its suspicions may have been aroused by a clumsy approach to the swim or the free offerings may have been dropped in at the wrong moment. Even if the carp's hiding in a safe area away from the bombardment of 2oz leads, it could become very agitated. If it starts to move about a lot faster, then beat a hasty retreat and creep back a couple of hours later to try again.

## Stalking at night

In murky water where you cannot study the carp's reactions, its sheer body-size will give it away as it pushes aside reeds or weeds. You may even be lucky enough to find a carp colouring the water as it searches for food. It is still possible to carry on stalking at night by casting a floating bait to fish patrolling the margins. On summer nights, carp often feed along the windward side of the lake. Sit down quietly and listen for the carp slurping for left-over bait or insects wedged among the reed stems.

If the wind has dropped sufficiently you will see oily ripples spreading out from the

## Floatfishing

Few of us devote much time to floatfishing because it demands constant alertness. But it is an excellent way of presenting a bait at short range among the pads or when stalking a bubbler. Any angler who invests time and effort in stalking will learn much more about carp fishing than those who sit behind their rods for days on end.

margins where the carp are feeding. Hold the rod with the tip just over the water's edge and lower a free-lined bait on the surface. Leave the bale arm open and grip the line between thumb and forefinger to feel for the take as the slurps get nearer.

## Long range tackle

The ability to cast those few extra yards can make all the difference in long range fishing. Inevitably that calls for a powerful set of tackle that will withstand the rigours of hurtling out heavy leads.

### Rod and reel

A stiff, fast tapered rod fits the bill for long distance and tip-actioned models built of Kevlar are justifiably popular. For the record, my 12ft Armalite blanks are fitted with seven rings for long casting purposes and the test curve rating is 2.25lb. They're fine for fishing at 100 metres but at extreme range — say 140 metres — then 13ft rods with a 2.5lb test curve are better.

I have tried all kinds of reel but can't find anything to match the Mitchell 300S for the evenness of its line lay. There is no bunching at the front or back and the wide spool can be overfilled quite safely to achieve extra distance.

### Line

Low diameter, pre-stretched lines are ideal for long casting and my preference is for Bayer Ultima Super Strong. Remember there's very little give with these monos and they are nothing like as abrasive resistant as standard lines.

A long range outfit with leger weights up to 3oz is a lethal weapon. Crack-offs could kill. For that reason, a shock leader or bumper as they're sometimes called *MUST* be used. A minimum of three rod lengths of non-stretched 15lb line is tied direct to the reel line with the stop swivel at the end. That gives a greater margin of safety when winding up to a big cast.

The most reliable knot for attaching the shock leader to the main line is a five-turn double blood. Trim the loose ends of the knot back to within 1cm (¹/₂in) and they

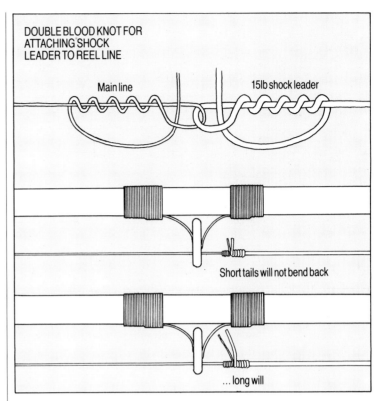

DOUBLE BLOOD KNOT FOR ATTACHING SHOCK LEADER TO REEL LINE

Main line    15lb shock leader

Short tails will not bend back

... long will

will be less likely to catch up in the rod rings and so impede line flow.

Shock leaders are also a good safety measure when fishing over gravel bars because the reel line near the leger weight is roughed up continually by the coarse bottom and will be severely weakened.

### Hooks

Suitable hooks for long range carping are the chemically sharpened Kamasan B980 and Drennan Super Specialist. They're similar designs with a small, neat barb and relatively wide gape for their size. But Kamasans are forged on a finer gauge of wire than Drennans which gives easier penetration at 100 metres where the power of the strike has little effect.

The drawback with the Kamasan B980 is that it is prone to spring out under severe pressure. This occurs with a light hook hold when only half the hook is buried beneath the skin and all the force is applied to the shank. The result is that the hook can pull out. Tie on the more robust Super Specialist if the pressure has to be piled on at long range to prevent a fish from reaching snags.

Probably the best reel ever made for long range retrieves. The Mitchell 300S gives absolutely perfect line lay (opposite).

These two patterns are fine on a hair-rig, but for eye-mounted and side-hooked baits you'll find the barbless Mustad Viking 94845 extremely efficient. In swims where it's possible to get away with a fine wired pattern the needle pointed Mustad Match Blue takes some beating for side-hooking.

## Long range methods

Now let's look at some long range methods, starting with the biggest problem posed by fishing at extreme distance: the effects of drift and drag on presentation.

### Drift and drag

Casting into a stiff cross wind puts a huge belly in the line which should be straightened out as much as possible before the bomb splashes down. This is done by braking the last few yards of the cast with the forefinger on the open spool, a technique known as feathering. But don't stop the line flow completely because the lead will suddenly bounce back on itself in mid-air, tangling the hooklink around the main line.

Once the bomb strikes the water, bury the line immediately by thrusting the rod tip beneath the surface, closing the bale arm and gently tightening up. Try not to overdo it and so move the lead.

Most nylon lines are naturally buoyant but will sink very quickly if the loaded spool is detached from the reel and left to soak overnight in a solution of washing-up liquid and cold water. One squirt of liquid to a couple of pints of water is the right level of dilution.

Once there's a straight line between bomb and rod tip the line clips and butt foam will keep it that way. But take the trouble to test every knot in your rig after three or four casts. Hurling the terminal tackle long distances imposes a lot of strain, particularly on the stop swivel knot which receives the most battering.

### Avoiding birdsnests

Over filling a spool with line to reach far-off swims inevitably results in a greater risk of birdsnests of tangled lines if stray loops are trapped within the coils. This won't happen if the line is wound back on the reel under constantly even pressure. Grip the line between forefinger and thumb on every retrieve. If you feel a slight burning sensation from the friction, run it through a small wad of towelling or foam.

During a lengthy scrap with a big carp some coils of line might be wound on so tightly that they squeeze through the layers beneath and become buried. This could damage the line and in extreme cases burst a plastic spool. The constrictions are usually released on the next few casts although the line will not flow from the spool as smoothly as usual.

The more acute problem is when a fish is hooked at maximum range and it runs off with an extra 25 metres or so of line. If this is recovered very tightly indeed and digs into the coils underneath, it must be freed later by recasting and walking backwards until the taut line peels from the spool.

## Accurate casting

The ability to cast consistently to the same prebaited spot is an obvious priority at any range. A short cut is to carefully select the weight of bomb that will just reach the swim with a powerful cast. That way you know a strong cast cannot overshoot the mark. A given weight should cast roughly the same distance every time if the propulsion remains constant. It is easier to judge the power of a cast by exerting full compression rather than holding back.

As a direction finder, line up with a bush, tree or bank of reeds on the far bank and aim to one side or the other to coincide with the prebaited area.

## Casting at night

If you can consistently cast to the right spot in daytime, there is no reason why you shouldn't achieve the same degree of accuracy at night. As a guide, once you've cast out mark the line in front of the rod tip for about 1m (3ft) with Tippex or coloured nail varnish. That will serve as an accurate distance marker for the night session. In fact, when the marked line shoots through the rings you will hear it clearly. Feather the line at the same time and you'll also be able to feel it. Immediately you hear or feel the marked line, brake the cast.

Direction finding is not so easy in darkness but if your casting style is the overhead thump make a note of your feet position during the day. Also, check how the lead hangs behind you before the cast is made. Finally, you can try a couple of trial casts with your eyes closed to confirm that you're on the mark. If you repeat the identical routine at night, then all should be well.

## Casting beneath trees

When casting tight to overhanging trees, clip on a much heavier weight than is required to reach the distance. The reason for this is that a heavier weight will obviously drop much faster when braked fairly hard as it reaches the correct range. The lead should dive very quickly, achieving the right sort of low trajectory to take it beneath the trees.

Feather the line as the lead nears the overhanging branches and slacken off completely once it hits the water. This ensures the bait is presented as far under the foliage as possible. A little dodge for dull conditions is to wrap silver paper around the bomb so that its flight path can be followed more clearly.

## Swim markers

Some carp hotspots are only a few feet square and in these cases it's a good idea to use a floating marker consisting of a spent film canister or a polyball. Attach the marker to a length of line that's slightly longer than the depth of the swim and tie a leger weight at the other end. Then secure the marker line to the reel line with PVA tape and cast out. There should be just enough time to manoeuvre the marker into position before the PVA melts. Don't forget to retrieve it at the end of the session!

## Long or short sessions?

The bivvy is the enemy of efficient carp fishing, at least for short sessions. If your hours on the bank are limited, then leave it at home. The disruption of moving swims with a bivvy is too great to contemplate when time is precious. A 50in umbrella provides all the protection necessary for a single night on the bank and if the fish start crashing out at the other end of the lake then you're mobile enough to take advantage.

If I'm on the bank for more than 48 hours and the swim allows me to cover most of the lake then I'll slip an overwrap on the brolly. The Kevin Nash 50in overwrap rolls up into a neat, light package and is easy to fit. You do not have to be a qualified tent erector as with many of the marquees made for carp anglers!

# PLAYING & HANDLING

Playing and handling need a careful, disciplined approach. The welfare of the carp must come first. But a great many opportunities are lost in the first phase of battle — the strike.

## The striking sequence

Responding to a sudden take which pours line from the reel requires a certain coolness in the heat of the moment. The sequence of actions leading up to the strike is: close the bale arm, check that no line has blown back around the reel and then tighten down, removing any slack until the bulk of the carp is felt. Always try to pull into a fish rather than snatching at it excitedly. Strike in one quick, smooth, movement taking the rod back over the shoulder.

A sideways strike is often advised in the belief that it gives more direct contact with the fish. Certainly it means there is less line to heave out of the water. But bankside obstructions make it impossible to execute on most waters and, frankly, it doesn't make a scrap of difference anyway.

In time, the smooth, disciplined striking sequence will become second nature and you'll do it almost without thinking, irrespective of whether you're hovering over the rods or disturbed while cat napping.

## Playing the fish

The measured approach does not end with striking — the limitations of the tackle must be uppermost in your mind while playing the fish. It is obviously futile heaving into a fast running carp with a 5lb hooklink but whatever the strength of the rig constant pressure must be maintained on the fish to avoid the line going slack.

Retrieve line by a pumping action. Wind the rod tip down towards the fish until it reaches the 10 o'clock position. Then hold the reel handle steady and pull the rod back over the shoulder to about 1 o'clock. Repeat this action until the fish is within netting range.

At some stage in the fight, the fish will probably win line against the pre-set clutch unless you screw it down tight and allow the reel to rotate backwards. Backwinding, as it's called, is the method preferred by most big fish anglers, despite much improved drag systems.

## Kiting

One tricky manoeuvre you'll certainly face is when a fish dashes straight towards the bank against a tight line and starts dictating matters — a problem known as kiting. To regain control, the carp's head must be pulled round by applying heavy side-strain so that it is pointing back towards you again. Keep the rod low to the water on a horizontal plane and this will increase the pressure against the side of the carp's mouth, forcing it to turn in an arc.

If the carp stubbornly resists this pressure and there's a danger of it running into snags, such as overhanging bushes in the margins, thrust the rod tip deep into the water to keep the line as near the lake bed as possible. That way there should be less

**Opposite:** Strong pole, soft mesh and 42in arms...it all adds up to a good landing net.

A

B

C

chance of it fouling trailing branches. Never slacken off when a fish is determinedly heading for a snag. Some anglers suggest that a slack line fools the fish into thinking the danger is over. But the carp will carry on crashing into the snag, slack line or not!

## Other common problems

Perhaps the trickiest problem you'll face while playing a carp is when it runs around the other side of an island. It's a shattering experience. All you can really do is maintain maximum pressure and keep the rod as low as possible.

Gravel bars that rise steeply from the depths are another serious hazard as carp often run along the bottom of troughs grating the line where it runs over the lip. Common sense should tell you to raise the rod up high, lifting as much line from the water as possible so it enters at a more acute angle. If there is a high bank behind then it's better to play the fish from there. Don't forget to take the precaution of fishing a snag leader when casting over bars of this kind.

If the carp manages to flee down the bank and almost out of sight it's usually best to follow by wading along the margins or lifting the rod over bankside bushes where deep water intervenes. An equally common problem is when a carp runs through other lines, which is certain to happen if you fish with three rods. Ask a neighbouring angler to reel in your other rods or drop the tips below the surface so the lines are sunk out of the way.

## Safe netting

When the fish is played out, don't let someone else net it for you unless you're confident of their ability. Too many carp have been lost at this crucial stage through inexperience. Sink the net well before steering the tired fish over it and don't try to scoop it out at full stretch. Despite this frequently repeated advice, you will still see the odd angler hold the end of the landing net handle with the rod hooped behind his back and the fish right out of reach. It's a hopeless stalemate but so easily avoided.

Always bring the carp right over the sunken net until its mouth is almost touching the spreader block. This guarantees it will go in first time. Do not stab at the fish or chase it with the net.

## The right net

It follows, of course, that the net itself must be right for the job. It should have a sturdy handle of between 5 and 6ft and arms of about 42in. Strong fibre glass is as good for the frame as lightweight boron and carbon because when the net is wet they all seem to weigh the same. A drawstring tensions the arms once they have been sprung into the aluminium spreader block. My block is a permanent fitting on the handle and an isotope is inset to aid the netting of fish in darkness.

A dual mesh net about 1.25m (4ft) deep should swallow the largest carp you're likely to meet. The beauty of the dual mesh design is that the micromesh in the base of the net gives the fish greater protection.

## Careful handling

The safest way of lifting a carp from the water is to gather the meshing together just below the arms of the landing net. This takes the strain off the arms and the spreader block.

Find a soft patch of ground on which to gently lay the carp or use a purpose-made unhooking mat. Whatever happens, do not put the fish down on hard ground. In an emergency use your bedchair or even spare clothing.

If the carp starts to thrash about at this stage do not attempt to pin it down against the hard ground. It is virtually impossible to restrain a carp in this manner without using excessive force and damaging the fish. Slip your hands underneath the fish instead and cradle it against your body. Again, avoid exerting undue pressure.

Moving carp with bare hands is fraught with potential dangers because a sudden kick from the fish could easily tear it free from your grasp. For that reason, it must be held as low to the ground as possible.

## The unhooking code

Exercise just as much care with the unhooking phase of the operation. Some carp have what I call a 'parrot' mouth —a hideous deformity caused by careless anglers. I feel quite sickened when I catch a carp in this condition. Because a hook penetrates point first with the barb holding it in place, it is obviously difficult to remove by pulling it out in the same direction as it went in. Tearing it free will remove flesh.

A fish hooked just inside the mouth or in the scissors will cause very few problems. It is a simple matter to grip the hook between thumb and forefinger and gently tease it out. When it is beyond the reach of the fingers, use a pair of forceps.

Where the real difficulties start to arise is when a hook is not easily freed because it is deeply embedded and has taken a very secure hold. In these cases you must cut the hooklink and then gently rotate the hook within the fleshy part of the mouth where it is secured and extract it point first. Removing it in this fashion prevents the barb being dug deeper into the skin. Snip the eye off the hook and repeat the same procedure when the hook has been driven deeply into the bony extremities of the lip.

If the hook has been swallowed so deep that it is out of sight, do not try to drag it back into view by the hooklink. It is better to leave well alone and cut the line as close to the hook as possible. The carp will eventually discard it.

Consistent deep hooking suggests the rig requires urgent adjustment. I have already described how to insert a short length of biro tube on the hooklink to stop bite-offs. But you may well solve the problem by simply shortening the hooklink.

A freshly captured carp inevitably draws other anglers to your swim to check on its size and it is asking for trouble if you lay your rod on the ground alongside the fish. Eventually someone is going to stand on it and that will ruin the day. Make a habit of propping the rod upright against a bush or leaving it in the rests with the bale arm open.

**Opposite:**
**Catch and return**
**A.** Nose up and over the sunk net first time.
**B.** Carefully unhook in the wet mesh over soft grass. Drape the mesh over the fish to protect it from the bright sun while the weigh bag is soaked in lake water and zeroed in on the scales.
**C.** Time for a quick trophy shot before release.

## Weighing the fish

Regardless of the type of scales you use, a purpose-made weighing sling is essential to provide the carp with the support it needs out of water. The sling should always be soaked in lake water to avoid removing protective mucus layers from the body of the fish.

Once the weigh sling is soaked, wring out the excess water and hang it on the scales to zero in the pointer. Follow this procedure and you will not have to worry about subtracting the weight of the sling once the carp has been on the scales.

Lay the carp on its side in the sling if there's any possibility that its body will be bent by its own weight once it is suspended from the scales. The weigh bags I prefer are made by Kevin Nash. The first accommodates carp up to about 30lb and is made from black nylon with heavy duty drawstring handles. It also has a built-in nose flap for extra security. My other bag is crescent shaped and will hold any carp that swims in this country.

Scales are once again a matter of personal choice but I favour the Salter tubular spring-balance that records up to 44lb

Easy to read dial scales. They leave no room for error.

and the Kevin Nash 56lb dial scales. Both are easy to read and zero in a wet weigh sling.

## Releasing and retaining

If the catch is not going to be photographed then it is best to release it immediately. Carefully lower the sling containing the carp into the lake and allow the base of the sling to sink free from the fish. Support the fish in an upright position with your hands, steadying it until it recovers and is ready to swim away. A freshly released carp frequently bolts off at great speed and its head must be pointed towards the middle of the lake otherwise it could injure itself by crashing into the margins.

### Choosing and using a sack

Fish caught at night can be retained until daylight for pictures if sacks are allowed on the water. There are some excellent designs on the market and I'd recommend that you purchase one made from industrial nylon rather than the keepnet type of close weave meshing.

Clearly, it must be possible for water to circulate freely through the weave of the sack for the safety of the carp. The best ones empty almost immediately when lifted from the water. Others drain very slowly and should not be used. Sacks are machined with top or side openings fastened by a drawstring and in some cases a heavy duty zip. A strong lanyard for staking out to a bank stick is another important design feature.

As with the weigh sling, sacks must be thoroughly soaked before they come into contact with a fish. Never put more than one carp in each sack. Doubling up results in two very sick-looking carp and a lot of loose scales in the bottom of the sack.

Always think carefully before positioning the sack. Deep, shady margins are the ideal resting place. At the other extreme, shallow water in direct sunlight on a summer's day is the worst possible spot imaginable. The fish will literally cook. Sacks need firmly staking out with a bank stick in an undisturbed area where the fish can lay up quietly, free from unnecessary stress. It goes without saying that carp should be sacked for the bare minimum of time.

## Taking a trophy shot

Everyone loves a trophy shot. If another angler is fishing near by it presents no problem. Set up the camera before removing the fish from the sack and spread out a wet mat or polythene sheet on which to lay it. Hold the carp close to your body and low to the ground. Pushing forward a fish at arm's length to create a more dramatic picture is foolhardy because of the risk to the fish if it should wriggle out of your grasp.

Never stand while photographing the catch or handle it with dry hands. If it's a very hot day, wring the sack over its head and body and keep it wet all the time it is out of the water. A carp dries out very rapidly with the sun on its back. The moment you feel the fish starting to tense itself for a vigorous flap of its tail, pull it close to your body and try to hold the head still, inserting a couple of fingers into its mouth. Take care to keep your fingers away from the entrance to the gill covers because the rakers inside are delicate and bleed easily.

When you're alone on the bank, photograph the fish on the mat with a set of scales or tape measure alongside for perspective. If you particularly want a trophy shot then most cameras have a time-delay mechanism. The method is to set up the camera on a tripod and mark the spot where you intend to kneel with a couple of rod rests. Focus on the rests and then you know that by kneeling in the same plane the picture of you and the fish should be crisp and sharp. When all is ready, set the self-timer and remove the fish from the water. In between shots, cover the carp up every time with your damp weigh sling or something similar.

Whenever you have to move a carp from one spot to another, it should always be carried in the weigh bag or sack rather than clutched in your arms. A carp out of water is at its most vulnerable. Always

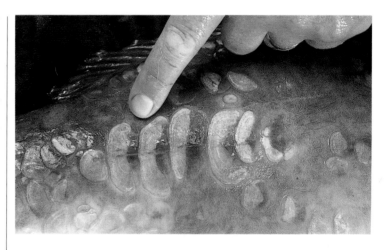

keep it wet, support and protect it. That's the way to make sure it goes back none the worse for its experience.

Photograph characteristic scale patterns such as this - or make a quick sketch -and it's easy to recognise recaptures.

## Record keeping

It's fascinating to monitor the development of individual fish, plotting their weight gains and losses and their vital statistics such as girth and length measurements. Recognising individual carp is relatively easy with the help of photographic records and notes.

Take common carp, for example, which on the face of it appear difficult to tell apart. On most fish you'll find an area of the scale pattern that is not uniform and quite distinctive. It could be an odd couple of slightly larger scales, a small patch of unevenly distributed scales or one or two might even be missing. The shape of the fins, especially the dorsal and tail, vary from carp to carp and are easily recognised from photographs. These features, with the back-up information of weight, length and girth, make it possible to distinguish one common from another.

Mirror carp are the easiest of the carp to tell apart. Scale pattern and size are extremely varied and many anglers recognise individual fish immediately without the benefit of their records. Indeed, some carp become so familiar because of repeated capture that they acquire names such as Popeye, Gertie Thirty or Lucky Leather. It seems sad, somehow, that these magnificent wild creatures should be labelled like comic strip characters.

# NIGHT & WINTER SESSIONS

Night fishing offers no short cuts to carp fishing success. The fish are likely to feed at any time of day or night on overpopulated waters and it is doubtful that the hours of darkness will be especially productive. In my experience, many of the rich, under-stocked or well-balanced waters rarely produce a take at night.

The advantage of night fishing is probably best felt on a long session — the sheer convenience of camping around the clock in the same spot must be less disturbing to the fish.

But there are fisheries where carp are forced to become nocturnal feeders. Obvious examples include waters shared with sports such as wind surfing where the fish are constantly pushed from one area to another during daylight. Their only chance to settle down and feed is at night. Heavily-fished waters where night fishing is restricted to a small syndicate might also produce more runs at night because of reduced pressure.

## Equipment for the night shift

A reliable pair of electronic bite indicators are essential for night fishing and isotopes fitted on the monkey climb indicators will also be appreciated in the inky blackness. It follows that the rods need positioning within easy reach of the bedchair.

## When temperatures tumble

Those who have never fished at night will be surprised at the marked temperature differences. For protection against the penetrating night chill, add extra layers of clothes or use a sleeping bag from which you can quickly scramble free. It is hilarious watching someone leaping along the bank like a giant mailbag, but I wouldn't recommend it! Good quality, ex-Army sleeping bags are modestly priced and many are equipped with full-length, quick release zips and waterproof underside.

If you only intend to fish the occasional night session then an ordinary garden lounger will serve as a bedchair but for more regular use invest in something like the Fox International model which has adjustable legs for uneven banks.

## Wet or dry

If I'm pretty certain it's not going to rain I use a waterproof cover to protect the sleeping bag and bedchair from damp leaving the umbrella in the holdall. The cover can easily be thrown off for a quick exit from the sleeping bag.

Some carp anglers suggest positioning the rods really close at hand making it possible to strike and play the fish without unzipping the sleeping bag. But I prefer to set up the rods about 1m (3ft) from the bedchair so I can get to my feet, slip on a pair of boots or shoes and concentrate on playing and landing the carp. It's no good staggering about from one foot to the other while climbing out of the sleeping bag and attempting to slip on your boots while in mid-battle! Wear something on your feet that can be pulled on very easily.

If it is wet then I recommend a pair of Derriboots a size larger than normal —

**Opposite:** Knowing the pitch well is vital in nightfishing. You can't afford to put a foot wrong in unfamiliar waters.

**Inset:** Midnight mirror from a Midlands pool. The red base to the tail confirms the richness of the bloodworm beds.

Early winter and no sign of the action slackening!

there's nothing more frustrating than struggling to pull on tight-fitting boots while the indicator is beating wildly on the butt ring. For shelter I find my 50in Wavelock umbrella keeps the entire bedchair dry without the need for the extra protection of a bivvy.

### Tackle — be prepared

It's good thinking to make up several ready-tied rigs in advance on which the baits are already mounted. You will find it much easier to replace a ready baited hooklink than to fiddle about in the darkness retying hooks and hairs. As well as spare rigs, carry a spare rod and reel made up in readiness just in case of a hopeless tangle.

All the tackle needs to be laid out neatly. I store most of mine in plastic ice-cream tubs which I leave under the bedchair. Scales, weighing sling and sack should also be left easily to hand.

Select a suitable spot for landing the carp and prop the net against a bush or reeds to prevent it being stepped on during the excitement of the fight.

Make sure you know the swim very well beforehand. The middle of the night is not the time to find you've got 2m (6ft) of water in the margins.

Try to anticipate any danger areas that the carp may head towards. When playing a fish crouch low to the water so that the bend of the rod is clearly silhouetted against the night sky. This will give you an idea of the direction in which the fish is moving.

Although I do not believe that lights have any adverse effects, they are very annoying to other anglers on the water. A shaded pen-torch is sufficient illumination and on most night sessions you will find your eyes quickly become accustomed to the dark. To maintain casting accuracy at night, pick out landmarks silhouetted against the skyline as direction markers.

Remember that sound travels well over water and is amplified at night. If you're fishing with a friend, conduct any conversations in whispers.

Finally, you'll hear many strange noises after dusk, mostly from bankside animals. Night fishing is not for the faint hearted. You'll be surprised at the number of men who have shaken in their boots and fled from a water during a night session — even though they might not admit to it!

## Winter carping

I suppose the most noticeable change between summer and winter carping is on the bank itself. In the warmer months the lakes are bursting with colour and life but winter transforms the scene into a drab, frequently hostile environment. Experience the pleasure of landing a carp against a backdrop of snow and all that changes! Suddenly the world becomes a much brighter place. The old myth that carp were virtually impossible to catch during winter has long been exploded. There is a marked initial drop in water temperature in late November and that's when winter carping starts in earnest.

### Winter feeding habits

This sudden fall, sometimes as much as 10 degrees Fahrenheit, induces the carp to change their feeding habits.

Immediately after the temperature drop they will stop feeding altogether but the effect is short-lived. Once the water temperature levels out again the carp resume a regular feeding cycle. The difference is that on most waters they'll probably only feed once or twice in every 24 hours.

The duration of these feeding periods is often less than one hour and on some waters you can almost set the clock by the feeding times while on others they become more spasmodic and unpredictable.

## How cold?

There is no ideal water temperature in winter. I have caught as many carp at 40 degrees F. as I have at 50 degrees which are the sort of readings you are likely to get at this time of year. But is there a temperature below which carp stop feeding completely? The lowest at which I've taken carp is 37 degrees F. and there's little chance to investigate much beyond that because most waters freeze over.

Although I enjoyed the years when I regularly logged air and water temperatures I'm not sure I learned a great deal! In a sense it can almost be detrimental. Let me explain. If I consistently caught carp at, say, 39 degrees F. but had not experienced a take at 37 F., then my confidence waned whenever the thermometer reading fell below 39. This meant I didn't try as hard as when temperatures were more favourable.

I know this may sound daft but you often get dejected when fishing alone in bleak conditions watching motionless indicators. Packing up and going home is a more inviting prospect than searching around for a feeding fish. With that thought in my mind, the thermometer was thrown in the dustbin several seasons ago and I now try hard regardless.

## Keeping warm

Whatever the conditions, there is no need to be uncomfortable on the bank. Specialist angling clothing has probably developed faster than the tackle itself. Thermal underwear and a one-piece wind- and water-proof suit will shield you against the harshest elements. The universally popular Moonboots have almost become standard issue for winter carping. Staying warm and dry means you can concentrate fully on putting a few fish on the bank.

## Coldweather hotspots

Winter hotspots will often be the same as summer ones, although I choose an area where there are significant differences in depth. This can take the form of a drop-off over a steep bar or something similar. The reason for doing this is that a series of sunny days in winter may well warm up the surface on bars and attract the carp out of deeper water alongside. As temperatures rise slightly, bloodworm and other food sources also become more active.

Fallen trees and overhanging bushes will draw carp in winter because they love a canopy over their heads. With less foliage to obstruct casting, it should prove possible to cast even further into these hiding places.

## Tackle

Tackle is much the same as in summer but on weedy waters where heavy line is normally required you can reduce the breaking strain as the growth dies back. Bite indicator systems also change very little although a slight nodding of the rod tip might be the only warning you will get and the set-up needs to be adjusted accordingly.

## Selecting a winter bait

You'll certainly need to rethink baits in winter. I have known carp to take a floater through ice holes but surface fishing is generally unproductive. Particles also become less effective, especially those that rely on natural oils as an attractor. As temperatures tumble, these oils become less soluble and therefore their attraction is reduced. Of all the particles, sweetcorn is the only one that seems to remain a consistent catcher through the bitter weather.

Luncheon meat and suspended crusts can score in winter when everything else fails. I often fish a large cube of meat on its own in a known hotspot or likewise a large chunk of crust suspended 7.5 to 10cm (3 to 4in) off the bottom.

Boilies remain the most consistent winter bait but steer clear of oil-based flavours unless used with tried and tested emulsifiers. I favour sweet flavours with good old standards such as strawberry, maple, dairy cream fudge and black cherry at the top of my list. I also use a concentrated sweetener to improve the attractiveness of the bait in cold conditions. Flavour levels in home-made baits are best increased by one or two per cent during the winter. Shelf-life baits benefit from being over-sprayed with the same flavour to give an extra boost.

## Feed sparingly

Having selected a winter bait, take care not to introduce too many free offerings because it is easy to over-feed the fish. During the shorter feeding spells, individual carp may only pick up between 10 and 20 boilies and if you put out any more than this the chances of a take will be decreased.

Where possible, it pays to introduce a small quantity of free offerings daily to get the carp used to feeding frequently on the bait. If you try to substitute this with a single weekly bait barrage you may well find 90 per cent of the boilies lying on the bottom uneaten for several days. These will proably go off and repel the carp.

I am happy with half-a-dozen free offerings in close proximity to my hookbait instead of a scattering. The trick is to try to pinpoint accurately a feeding area and stick to it. If any free offerings need to be introduced they should be placed as close as possible to the hookbait.

## Rivals for the baits

During the hard winter months, seagulls and tufted ducks develop an intense liking for boilies. They learn to pick out the sound of a catapult and associate it with a meal. Seagulls are capable of snatching baits from the surface of the water or in mid-air — and you're never really sure if any free offerings have actually got through to the fish below! This is when stringer rigs really come into their own. My two favourite methods are the exploding stringer system or small bunches of boilies tied on with PVA thread.

## Keep cool!

I don't know if it's my imagination playing tricks, but carp seem to fight much harder in winter and their colours are truly vibrant. Try to avoid touching them with warm hands — I'm sure it's an unpleasant sensation for the fish. Cool your hands in the lake beforehand. It might make you wince but fish care comes first!

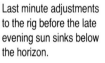

Last minute adjustments to the rig before the late evening sun sinks below the horizon.

# BAIT IDEAS

There is enormous satisfaction in making up your own baits and experimenting with different ingredients and flavours. But it's no good proceeding blindly – the end product must be a balanced bait.

## Boilies

In theory it is possible to grind up or liquidise any edible substance, mix it with a few eggs, roll it into balls and boil it. But over the seasons certain ingredients have emerged as consistent winners and they are recognised as the mainstay of a boiled bait.

### Winning ingredients

Here is a checklist of the best ingredients:

CASEIN — the base ingredient of many high-nutritional-value (HNV) baits. Powdered casein is the main protein extracted from raw milk. I'd recommend New Zealand lactic casein which is very fine at 80 per cent mesh and 95 per cent protein. It can form as much as 50 per cent of the bait's dry ingredients.

CALCIUM CASEINATE — another very fine powder which is a soluble form of casein. It has a protein content of 95 per cent and makes up between 10 and 40 per cent of the base mix.

SODIUM CASEINATE — much lighter than calcium caseinate, which makes it excellent for mixing up floaters or to give boilies extra buoyancy. Protein level is about 95 per cent. Take care not to introduce too much of this powder into the mix unless you want it to float — 10 to 20 per cent is about right.

LACTALBUMIN — should always be used with caseins and caseinates as it helps achieve a well-balanced HNV bait. Try to buy lactalbumin originating from New Zealand. It will have a protein content of about 86 per cent and should form between 10 and 20 per cent of the mix.

WHEAT GLUTEN — without any doubt this is the most effective binding agent. Various grades are obtainable, with protein levels from 80 to 90 per cent. Between 10 and 20 per cent of the mix is sufficient to bind most powders together.

SOYA FLOUR — made from ground soya beans. This has a fairly high oil content and should only be used in small quantities if you want to maintain the protein level of the HNV bait. Available with a protein content of between 40 and 50 per cent. Around 10 per cent of soya flour is more than adequate.

SOYA ISOLATE — the isolated protein of the soya bean which again helps achieve a well-balanced HNV bait. Should be used at a level of 10 to 20 per cent of the mix. Protein content up to 90 per cent.

WHEATGERM — often overlooked these days but a favourite of mine. High in fibre and vitamin content, it has a distinctive smell all of its own. Very useful as the roughage part of the bait. Best used as between 10 and 20 per cent of the mix.

VITAMEALO — not particularly high in protein but effective with sweet baits. Has a nice creamy smell and I like to use it at about 15 to 20 per cent of a medium protein mix. Vitamealo's protein content is about 30 per cent.

EQUIVITE — a vitamin and mineral replacer mainly used for horses. This was

the first of a long line of substitutes copied by leading carp bait suppliers. Should constitute no more than 10 per cent of the mix.

PROTEX — textured vegetable protein with strong smell that blends well with meaty-type flavours. Forms up to 10 per cent of the mix.

PRUTEEN — single-celled animal protein that was once hailed as a replacement for the milk proteins. It consistently catches carp but I have yet to prove that it is any better than the milks. Very fine powder with a protein level of 73 per cent and can make up as much as 75 per cent of the bait's ingredients.

WHITEFISH MEAL — I hold fish meal in high regard. The consistency varies from batch to batch but the protein content is usually 66 per cent and it can form up to 30 per cent of the base mix.

SHRIMP MEAL — most shrimp meals are too coarse to be used straight from the packet and require grinding. They should have a protein content of 50 per cent and constitute about 30 per cent of the mix. Wherever possible buy whole shrimp meal.

ANCHOVY MEAL — my favourite fish meal but difficult to obtain. Most was imported

from Argentina. It is possible to obtain dried anchovies that you can grind up but they are not as good as the real thing. If you can find this product it will be expensive but the investment is worthwhile. Protein content is up to 60 per cent and the meal can form up to 30 per cent of the ingredients.

CODLEVINE — vitamin supplement which is a derivative of fish offal. Very useful with fish meals and around 10 per cent of the base mix will be sufficient.

Other proven bait ingredients are as follows: liver powder, beef meal, feather meal, meat and bone meal, molasses meal, hemp meal, salmon and trout fry, trout pellets, sardine meal, mackerel meal, sand-eel meal, capelin, maize meal, peanut meal, rice powder and semolina.

Bird food also makes excellent boilies. My favourites include Robin Red, Nectar Blend, PTX, Sluis Universal and Sluis Mynah.

## Home-made boilie mixes

To achieve a balanced bait that will be of lasting appeal to the carp, you must use combinations of the ingredients listed above in the correct proportions. Most boilie mixes are made up in amounts of 10oz and you will find the following recipes produce excellent results:

RECIPE A: 5oz casein, 2oz lactalbumin, $1^1/_2$oz calcium caseinate, 1oz gluten, $^1/_2$oz Equivite.

**The right way to make a boilie**

**A.** The utensils and ingredients for a 10oz mix. Suggested breakdown is 4oz casein, 1oz lactalbumin, 2oz calcium caseinate, 1oz gluten, $1^1/_2$oz soya isolate, $^1/_2$oz vitamin and mineral supplement.
**B.** Whisk up eggs, flavour, colour and sweetener in the bowl.
**C.** Add dry premixed powders.
**D.** Roll out the mix into sausage sized strips.
**E.** Rub margarine into hands and break off two slugs from roll.
**F.** The correct way to roll boilies – two at a time –to produce neat, perfectly round balls.
**G.** Boil for two minutes in sieve.
**H.** Place hot baits on towel to dry off.

G

H

RECIPE B: 4oz casein, 2oz lactalbumin, 1oz sodium caseinate, 1oz soya isolate, 1oz Vitamealo, ½oz gluten, ½oz Equivite.

RECIPE C: 5oz Nectar Blend, 2oz PTX, 1½oz Robin Red, 1oz gluten, ½oz wheatgerm.

RECIPE D: 3oz whitefish meal, 2oz shrimp meal, 2oz anchovy meal, 2oz gluten, 1oz Codlevine.

RECIPE E: 4oz semolina, 4oz ground rice, 1oz gluten, 1oz Vitamealo.

## Ready-mixed boilies

If you don't fancy making up boilie mixes yourself, there are some very good ready-mix packs on the market. Buy the best available. Those I'd recommend are Crafty Catcher products, Geoff Kemp's Bait Ingredients and Rod Hutchinson's Catchum baits.

## The right way to make a boilie

The utensils you will need are a mixing bowl, kitchen scales, wooden mixing spoon, egg whisk, large saucepan and a flour sieve.

Let us assume that the ingredients are casein, calcium caseinate, lactalbumin, wheat gluten, soya isolate and Equivite. There is also a liquid flavour and concentrated sweetener plus a powdered colour. Six large eggs bind the mix together and you will need a tub of margarine to help roll the bait between the palms of your hands.

The first step is to beat the eggs in a bowl, adding the flavour, colour and sweetener. Always follow the manufacturer's recommended dosage. In this mix it is 7ml of Fruitex flavour and 1ml of concentrated sweetener.

Weigh out the dry ingredients and mix them well together. You should always have more than enough dry mix at hand for the number of eggs you intend to use. Slowly add the dry mix to the beaten eggs, stirring with the wooden spoon until it is the consistency of thick soup. Leave the mix to stand for about five minutes to allow the dry ingredients to completely absorb the eggs. This will produce a very even consistency and prevents the mix drying out during rolling.

Next, knead the mix together and split it into two or three even lumps. Roll these into large balls. Select a suitable clean working-surface on which to roll the baits and grease it with margarine or lard, working some into the palms of your hands at the same time. Break a chunk

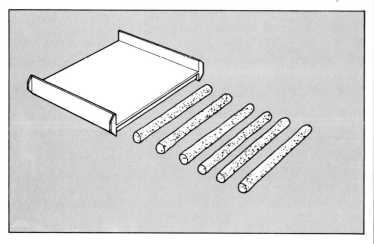

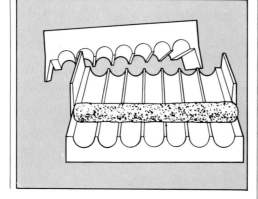

The labour-saving Rollaball system in operation. Sausages are formed on the rolling table and then sliced into neat balls.

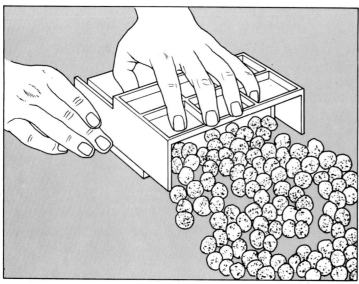

of bait from one of the large balls and roll it out into a long, thin sausage shape of about the same diameter as you require the finished boilies.

Carry on rolling sausages until you have used up all the large balls. Then pinch a couple of slugs of bait from a sausage and roll them simultaneously — one between the palms and the other at the base of your fingers. Rolling baits in this manner between greasy hands will produce consistently round boilies and prevent the mix sticking.

Once you have rolled out the whole mix, let the baits stand for another five minutes until they've got a slight skin which stops them sticking together.

Next, place a handful of baits in the flour sieve and lower them into a saucepan of boiling water. It is vital that the water is kept vigorously on the boil otherwise the baits will become very soggy and possibly even break apart. The sieve should hold about 25 or so half-inch diameter boilies — cram in any more and the water will tend to go off the boil.

With this particular mix, boil the baits for approximately two minutes then turn them out on to a sheet of newspaper or kitchen towel to dry off. The longer you leave them drying the harder they'll become.

If you are making baits for the freezer, don't wait for them to dry off once they have boiled. Put them straight into the freezer bag still steaming. This will trap water inside and stop the boilies drying out after thawing.

To produce pop-ups, put aside some baits after rolling and bake them in a microwave or oven to make them float.

### Labour savers

There are devices to make boilie production less time consuming, most notably the Gardner Rollaball system. Once the bait sausages have been squeezed out on the rolling table, they are stretched out two or three at a time along the rolling grooves. The top half of the Rollaball is then fitted and slid horizontally across the bottom. This cuts through the baits and rolls them at the same time.

## How to bake floating cake

To prepare a cooked floater, mix the following dry ingredients together: 4oz casein, 2oz sodium caseinate, 2oz lactalbumin, 1oz soya isolate, 1oz gluten, 2 teaspoonfuls baking powder.

Beat up a dozen large eggs, adding colour and flavour at the same time. Then pour the beaten eggs into the dry mix, whisking well to give a sloppy texture. Try to beat in as much air as possible as this produces cake with a nice consistency. Pour the mix into a pre-greased baking tin and slowly cook in the oven for up to 90 minutes until a crust is formed. After baking, the texture should be like that of a light Madeira cake. Cut the cake up into suitable sizes for fishing.

## What the future holds

When I look back it doesn't seem to have taken us very long to have reached the present stage of bait development. In some respects I think it has happened too fast. Many things have been overlooked and no single idea has been taken to its limit. We have advanced in leaps and bounds, trying to improve on the last successful idea before it ever became fully exploited.

Many anglers believe we have reached a threshold in bait development — but I think not. I am sure that boilies will be with us for many years to come but I am equally convinced there are dramatic developments just around the corner. We could well see an encapsulated liquid bait coming on the market very soon. It is almost like the perfect pill syndrome: all that is needed to sustain life contained in a single, soluble capsule!

New particles appear every season. Who would have thought ten years ago of using Brazil or cashew nuts? Carp anglers with inquiring minds will continue to explore new areas and that is what makes this magnificent fish so challenging. There is always something fresh to learn.

If you're completely fresh to carpfishing it pays to concentrate on just a couple of easy waters in your first season. The size of the fish does not really matter - it's more important to gain experience of handling the tackle and the carp themselves. Getting it right from the start will pay dividends in later seasons.

It's good to know that the novice can net a 20-pounder on his first trip but for every successful first-timer there will be a hundred frustrated anglers trying to cope with the rigours of tackling a difficult water.

The ideal lake on which to start is one where the carp are hungry and willing to accept most types of baits which are well presented. This allows a broad range of techniques to be tried and avoids the trap of becoming a single-method angler. Once you've got this experience under your belt it's time to branch out to the more difficult lakes containing bigger fish. Avoid joining too many waters at once — you'll never get to know a lake if you're forever racing from one to the other.

It's wise to join one of the specialist groups. Both the Carp Society and Carp Anglers' Association stage regular meetings where you can meet like-minded anglers and gain information about waters. Contact the Carp Society by writing to the secretary at 33, Covert Road, Hainault, Ilford, Essex. The Carp AA's address is Heywood House, Pill, Bristol BS20 OAE.

There are hundreds of carp fisheries in Britain and the following is a cross-section that will hopefully put you in touch with the fish of your dreams:

Craichlaw Loch, Newton Stewart, Wigtownshire. Six acre water controlled by the proprietors of Palakona Guest House at 30, Queen St, Newton Stewart. Telephone 0671-2323.

Fellgate Fishery, Gateshead. Three acre lake, well stocked with mid-doubles. Day tickets from Steve Sloan, telephone 091-489-6919.

Pilsworth Fishery, Heywood, Lancashire. Nine acre lake well stocked with doubles. Day tickets on bank.

Nostell Priory, Wakefield, Yorkshire. Three lakes ranging from six to 26 acres. All well stocked with carp to more than 20 lb. Day tickets from the fishing lodge. Telephone 0924-863562.

Tilery Lake, Broomfleet Tile Factory, near Hull. Well stocked 30 acre clay pit with carp to around 25 lb. Permits from Hull and District AA.

Chorlton Water Park, Maitland Avenue, Chorlton, Manchester. Park lake of 19 acres containing mid-doubles. Day or season tickets from warden's hut or on bank.

Redesmere, Capesthorne Hall Estate, Siddington, Cheshire. Famous water covering 45 acres. Details of club membership from Stoke-on-Trent AS, Lynton, 5, Kingsfield Oval, Basford, Stoke-on-Trent, Staffordshire.

Bridgewater Canal controlled by Warrington AA, Cheshire. Well stocked with carp to mid-doubles. Association also controls Grey Mist Mere holding carp to over 20lb. Contact Warrington AA at PO Box 71, Warrington WA1 1LR. Telephone Runcorn 716238.

Higham Farm, Alfreton, Derbyshire. Complex of four lakes between two and three acres stocked with carp to 20 lb. Permits from Higham Farm Hotel, Old Higham, Alfreton, Derbyshire.

Chapel Boating Lake, Skegness, Lincolnshire. Stocked with fish to more than 20 lb but only opens from mid-March to the end of October. Day tickets from John Cook on 0754 72631.

The Poplars, North Scarle, Lincoln. Two one acre lakes holding carp to 20 lb plus. Permits from Mr Day on 052 227338.

Sheepy Lake, Sheepy Magna, Leicestershire. This 5. 50 acre water is well stocked with carp to 20lb plus. Tickets on the bank.

Waveney Valley Lakes, Wortwell, Suffolk. Famous complex of eight lakes ranging from two to five acres and offering carp to 36lb. Day tickets on the bank.

Ditchford Lakes, off A45 at Rushden, Northants. Run jointly by two local clubs. Two well stocked lakes and stretch of River Nene. No day tickets. Season tickets from Jack Leach tackle shop, 26, Church St, Rushden.

Little Paxton Fishery, St Neots, Cambridgeshire. Four lakes controlled by Redlands, three of which are stocked with carp to 26lb. Tickets available from Ian May, 5, Hayling Avenue, Little Paxton, Huntingdon, Cambridgeshire PE 19 4HG.

Woolpack Fisheries, Cow Lane, Godmanchester, Cambridgeshire. Two carp lakes well stocked with fish to 20 lb. Approximately 10 acres. For full information contact Bill Chillingworth, The Cottage, St Peters Street, Caxton, Cambridgeshire. Telephone Caxton 593.

Kingsbury Water Park, Kingsbury, Warwickshire. Gibsons Pool, three acre pool stocked with 130 doubles, some over 20lb. Season ticket only. Pine Pool, three acres stocked mainly with small carp - day tickets from Park Visitor Centre, Bodymoor Heath Lane, Sutton Coldfield B76 ODY.

Cuttle Mill, Wishaw, Sutton Coldfield, Birmingham. Two pools offering large head of 20-pounders. Day tickets available. For more details contact Tony Higgins on 0827-872253.

Withy Pool, Henlow Camp, Bedford SG 16 6EA. Old, privately owned brick pit of 2. 50 acres containing fish to more than 37lb. New three-quarter acre lake has carp to 20lb. More information from fishery owner Kevin Maddocks.

South Essex Carp Fisheries, South Ockendon, Essex. Gravel pits stocked with carp to 30lb. Anglers must become honorary members before being issued with day or night permits. Full information from the controller, Tom Coster, 723, Longbridge Road, Dagenham, Essex RM8 2DD.

Claydon Lake, Steeple Claydon, near Winslow, Bucks. Best known for its catfish but contains double-figure carp and occasional 20-pounder is taken. Season tickets from Leighton Buzzard AC, 52, Mentmore Road, Linslade, Bedfordshire. Same club controls Tiddenfoot Pit, Mentmore Road, Leighton Buzzard which holds a good head of commons and mirrors.

Llandrindod Wells Lake, Llandrindod Wells, Powys. Heavily stocked 16 acre water and the odd 20-pounder is reported. Tickets from the Boathouse Cafe at the side of the lake.

Blue Lake, Waun-Y-Pound Industrial, Estate, Ebbw Vale, Gwent. Four acre reservoir holding 20-pounders. Can be fished on a season ticket from BSC AC, 52, Bethcar Street, Ebbw Vale, Gwent.

Roath Park Lake, Cardiff. Four acre lake with plenty of doubles. Day tickets on bank.

Anwell, Stanstead Abbots, Ware, Hertfordshire. Leisure Sport controlled pits of seven and three acres. A 30-pounder has been reported. Tickets from LSA, Thorpe Park, Staines Road, Chertsey, Surrey.

Holwell Hyde Lake, Cole Green, Welwyn Garden City. Redland water of two acres containing carp to 25 lb. Day tickets on bank.

Aldermaston, Paices Hill, near Reading, Berkshire. Leisure Sport complex of seven lakes with fish to mid-twenties. Tickets from LSA, Thorpe Park, Staines Road, Chertsey, Surrey.

Savay Lake, Harefield, Denham, Buckinghamshire. Probably the most productive big carp fishery in the land with numerous 20-pounders and a well known common of 39 lb nicknamed Sally. Redland controlled pit of 60 acres can be fished on a day ticket which must be purchased before fishing from Peverills Newsagents, 3, Moorhall Road, Harefield or Balfours Newsagents, 12, Station Parade, Denham.

Harefield Carp Lake, Harefield, Middlesex. The pit that is still being worked contains a good head of carp including probably the biggest fully scaled mirror in the country at 31 lb. This William Boyer controlled water can be fished on a limited, numbered permit. For details contact William Boyer Fishing, Trout Road, West Drayton, Middlesex.

Staines Road, Wraysbury. Another famous Leisure Sport complex of three pits. The four acre water is a difficult venue but contains fish over 40 lb. Tickets from LSA at the address listed previously.

Rodney Meadow, near West Drayton, Middlesex. William Boyer venue with numbers of 20 lb carp and the odd 30-pounder. Limited ticket water. Contact William Boyer Fishing, Trout Road, West Drayton, Middlesex.

Farlows Lake, near Iver, Buckinghamshire. Large, mature gravel pit with lots of doubles and several 20-pounders. Day tickets on the bank. Another water controlled by William Boyer.

Brooklands Lake, Dartford, Kent. A 20 acre gravel pit heavily stocked with doubles and 20-pounders. Very busy water. Day tickets on the bank.

Darenth Lakes, Dartford, Kent. Leisure Sport fishery comprising four pits between 3 and 18 acres. Popular venue well stocked with doubles and 20-pounders. Two of the waters contain 30 lb carp. For more information contact Leisure Sport Angling, Thorpe Park, Staines Road, Chertsey, Surrey.

Horton Kirby Lakes, Dartford, Kent. Three pits stocked with plenty of doubles and several well known 20-pounders. Day tickets on the bank.

School Pool, Faversham, Kent. Gravel pit of 18 acres with most famous inhabitant being 'She' who is regularly caught and recorded at weights up to 35 lb. Day tickets on bank.

Britten's Pond, Salt Box Road, Jacobs Well, Guildford, Surrey. Easy and popular small pond with plenty of fish under 10 lb. A few carp to mid-doubles also prsent. Permits on bank.

Cutt Mill, Puttenham, near Farnham, Surrey. The most popular carp fishery in Surrey. A seven acre pool with a reasonable head of 20-pounders. Best fish from the water was weighed at just under 30 lb. Season tickets from Farnham AS membership secretary, The Creel, 26, Station Road, Aldershot, Hants.

Trilakes, Yateley Road, Sandhurst, Surrey. Two gravel pits totalling about ten acres. Biggest lake offers specimens to more than 30 lb including a superb common. Can be fished on a day ticket obtained from the fishing hut before starting.

Old Bury Hill Lake, Dorking. Attractive 12 acre water holding carp to 30lb and plenty of mid-doubles. Day tickets on bank.

Yateley Pits, near Staines, Middlesex. Leisure Sport complex of 13 waters. Most popular is pit No. 11 (match lake) which is well stocked with 20-pounders. Pit No. 4 (north lake) contains the second largest carp ever landed in this country scaling 45 lb 12 oz. Pit No. 9 (car park lake) contains no more than eight fish but one of them is Heather the Leather weighing more than 40 lb. The other water of interest to carp anglers is pit No. 12(Copse) which is very difficult but has produced carp to just under 40 lb. A difficult complex of pits representing a tremendous challenge for experienced carpmen. Tickets from Leisure Sport Angling, Thorpe Park, Staines Road, Chertsey, Surrey.

Hollybush Lane Lakes, Farnborough, Hampshire. Redlands complex of gravel pits. Fish to more than 20 lb are stocked in these waters. Day tickets from local tackle shops or the newsagents at 201, Lynchford Road close to the fishery. Pit No. 5 can only be fished on a season ticket obtainable from Graham Rowles, Old Bury Hill, Dorking, Surrey.

Broadlands Lake, Romsey, Hampshire. A 27 acre lake alongside the M27 motorway on the outskirts of Southampton. Well stocked with doubles and available on 24 hours or day tickets. More information from Mark Simmonds on Southampton 733167.

Gunville Pond, Carisbrooke, Isle of Wight, Hampshire. Heavily stocked three acre lake. Day or season tickets from most tackle shops on the island.

Dunwear Ponds, Bridgwater, Somerset. Four pits to 20 acres. All ponds are heavily stocked with singles and the odd double. Season or day tickets from Bridgwater AA, 7, Webbers Way, Puriton, Bridgwater, Somerset TA7 8AS.

Combwich Pond, Combwich, , near Bridgwater. A 25 acre pit containing fair head of doubles. Ticket details as for Dunwear Ponds.

Tockenham Reservoir, Lyneham, Wiltshire. Well stocked eight acre reservoir containing the odd double to 20 lb. Season tickets from Bristol and District AA, 16, Lansdowne View, Kingswood, Bristol.

Anglers Paradise fishing holiday complex. Seven lakes, three of which hold carp. The main carp pool has 180 doubles to 20lb plus. Contact Zyg Gregorek, The Gables, Winsford, Halwill Junction, Beaworthy, Devon. Telephone Beaworthy(040922) 559.

Lower Tamar Lake, Bideford, Devon. Most carp in this 40 acre reservoir are singles but there is the chance of an odd 20-pounder. Day tickets from a self-service unit adjacent to the dam.

College Reservoir, Falmouth, Cornwall. This 38 acre reservoir has a good head of 20-pounders. Day tickets from the self-service unit in the Argal carp park on the opposite side of the road to College.

Shillamill Lakes, Lanreath, Looe, Cornwall. Three small lakes with fish to 35lb plus. Permits available from John Facey, Shillamill Lakes, Lanreath, Looe, Cornwall. (0503 20271). No Close Season.

# index